UNMUTE COURAGEOUS CATALYSTS

Leading South Africa Beyond Historical Trauma and Fragmentation

LINDOKUHLE T H KHOZA

Copyright © 2024 by Lindokuhle T H Khoza.

All rights reserved. No part of this book may be used or reproduced in any form whatsoever without written permission except in the case of brief quotations in critical articles or reviews.

Printed in the Republic of South Africa.

For more information, or to book an event, contact :
(lindo@lindbong.co.za)
http://www.lindbong.co.za

Book design by (Lindbong Development Group)

ISBN: 978-0-7961-9021-5 (print book)
ISBN : 978-0-7961-9022-2 (e-book)
First Edition: August 2024

Dedication

This book is dedicated to the **fearless catalysts**, both celebrated and unsung, who have dared to dream of a unified South Africa, unshaken by the shadows of our troubled past. To those who face the deep-seated injustices of our time with relentless courage, and who continue to fight for a future defined by unity, justice, and unyielding hope.

To my **family**, whose unwavering support and belief in this vision have been the foundation of my journey. Your encouragement has turned obstacles into steppingstones, and your faith has sustained me through every challenge.

To my **Lord and Savior, Jesus Christ**, whose radical teachings and example of love, justice, and sacrificial service inspire me daily. This work is dedicated to the transformative power of the Gospel of the Kingdom of God and the absolute sovereignty of our Creator over all creation. Your principles are the compass guiding our quest for a just and reconciled society.

To the **political activists, transformation agents, and champions of social justice and reconciliation** who challenge the status quo with unrelenting commitment to equity. Your tireless efforts to address systemic inequities and advocate for righteous change are the heartbeat of our movement for societal transformation.

To the **entrepreneurs and marketplace leaders** who drive economic innovation, create opportunities, and champion ethical practices that honor God's sovereignty. Your dedication to reshaping our economic landscape is crucial in the journey toward a thriving and just society.

To the **academics and next-generation leaders**, whose intellect, vision, and passion are essential in shaping the future. Your insights and leadership are critical in pioneering new ideas and driving systemic change.

To the **frustrated and fed-up**, who have grown weary of the status quo and are ready to challenge it. Your discontent is a catalyst for action, and your determination to see a better South Africa is a powerful force for change.

To all those in **service to our nation**—whether in public service, community work, or various other forms of contribution—your dedication is a testament to the spirit of collective effort required to rebuild and renew our society. May this book ignite within each of us a fire of audacious courage, profound compassion, and an unwavering commitment to a just, unified South Africa, under the sovereign authority of God.

Preface

Unmute Courageous Catalysts: Leading South Africa Beyond Historical Trauma and Fragmentation is more than just a title; it is a radical and unyielding call to action for every South African. It demands that you refuse to remain passive amidst the turmoil and division that have plagued our nation for far too long. This book is not merely a reflection of my journey but a direct challenge to all of us to rise up and lead with audacious courage, uncompromising justice, and a relentless pursuit of unity.

Faith as the Foundation

Faith is the bedrock of my journey and this book's foundation. Guided by the principles of Biblical justice, love, and compassion, we are called to act decisively and humbly in the face of the profound challenges our nation endures. Micah 6:8— "to act justly and to love mercy and to walk humbly with your God"—is not just a scripture but a divine mandate that fuels our mission. This faith-driven conviction demands that you confront systemic injustices, embrace reconciliation, and work tirelessly for the greater good. This book is a testament to the power of redeeming grace of God as manifested in the ultimate sacrifice of Christ and faith in Him as a catalyst for societal transformation, urging us to embrace these principles as a guide for our actions.

Political Persuasions and a Vision for Justice

Political convictions are inseparable from our faith. Our vision extends beyond the superficial, aiming for a governance system marked by absolute transparency, unwavering accountability, and a commitment to inclusivity and equity. This book challenges the status quo, demanding a departure from mediocrity and apathy in political leadership. It calls for us to break from convention, to embrace bold, visionary policies that confront economic disparities, foster social cohesion, and promote sustainable development. The call to action is clear: rise above complacency, lead with integrity, and enact transformative change.

A Passion for Transformation

At its core, this book embodies a fierce passion for seeing South Africa transcend its historical traumas and current divisions. My journey has been a profound exploration of our nation's struggles, its resilience, and its boundless potential for renewal. It is a passionate cry for a future where unity prevails over division, and where justice overcomes the legacy of past injustices. This book acknowledges the scars of our past but focuses intently on the promise of a future where every South African can thrive in a just and equitable society.

Empowering the Next Generation

A cornerstone of this vision is an unshakeable belief in the transformative potential of South Africa's next generation. This book is dedicated to you, the young leaders, academics, and organic intellectuals who dare to defy the status quo and envision a brighter future. It is an urgent call to nurture your talents, support your ambitions, and equip you with the tools necessary to become powerful catalysts for change. You are not only our future but are pivotal to the transformation we seek today.

Empowering Change Agents

Unmute Courageous Catalysts serves as a radical manifesto for change, designed to inspire and empower everyone—from political leaders and community activists to business professionals and everyday citizens. It delves into practical strategies for economic empowerment, educational reform, mental health, and cultural sensitivity. This book provides actionable insights and urges you to engage deeply with these issues, fostering a more just and inclusive society. It is an invitation to lead with purpose and impact, to be audacious in the face of challenges, and to actively contribute to meaningful societal transformation.

A Collective Effort

In South Africa, courageous catalysts—those bold individuals and groups who have the potential to drive transformative change—are indeed present. Yet, their voices have often been silenced by a myriad of factors. Historical traumas, systemic inequalities, and persistent socio-political fragmentation have conspired to mute these agents of change. Economic disparities and entrenched power structures stifle innovation and activism, while cultural and racial tensions inhibit the unity necessary for collective progress. Despite these challenges, the resilience and resolve of these catalysts persist, waiting for an opportunity to be unmuted and to lead the nation toward healing and growth.

This book is more than a narrative; it is a call to action. It calls upon all of us, the courageous catalysts, to unmute ourselves and step into our roles as leaders of transformation.

Furthermore, it is a rallying cry to academic and church leaders, parents, educators, community leaders, and anyone with access to both current catalysts and next-generation pioneers. It urges us to facilitate and expedite the unmuting process, empowering and developing these courageous individuals. By doing so, we can harness their transformative potential and guide South Africa beyond its historical trauma and fragmentation.

The path to transformation is a collective endeavor that demands the active participation of all. This book is not just a call to read but a summons to act. It challenges us to unmute our voices, confront persistent injustices, and play a vital role in shaping a more equitable and harmonious nation. It is a rallying cry for all of us to embrace our roles in this monumental task of rebuilding our society with courage and integrity.

A Future of Hope and Unity

As you engage with the chapters of this book, let them be a source of inspiration and conviction. Reflect deeply on the principles presented, let them ignite your passion, and propel you into action. Lead with courage, challenge injustice, and contribute meaningfully to our collective journey toward healing and transformation. Together, let us envision and work toward a future where every South African thrives, where the wounds of our past are healed, and where unity and justice form the bedrock of our society.

This is more than a book; it is a call to arms for every South African willing to confront the challenges of our time with relentless courage and radical conviction. Embrace this challenge with the passion and urgency it demands and join us in forging a new path for our nation.

In faith, hope, and unwavering commitment,

Lindokuhle T. H. Khoza

Table of Contents

DEDICATION 2

PREFACE 3

CHAPTER 1: UNDERSTANDING THE CONTEXT 7

CHAPTER 2: CULTIVATING EMPATHY AND COMPASSION 12

CHAPTER 3: DEVELOPING RESILIENCE IN SOUTH AFRICA 17

CHAPTER 4: EFFECTIVE COMMUNICATION 23

CHAPTER 5: LEADING WITH COURAGE 28

CHAPTER 6: EMBRACING DIVERSITY AND INCLUSION 34

CHAPTER 7: BUILDING THRIVING AND COHESIVE COMMUNITIES 41

CHAPTER 8: PROMOTING AND CHAMPIONING RACIAL RECONCILIATION 46

CHAPTER 9: EMPOWERING THE YOUTH 53

CHAPTER 10: FAITH-INSPIRED LEADERSHIP: TRANSFORMING SOCIETY WITH UNSHAKABLE CONVICTION 62

CHAPTER 11: POLITICAL LEADERSHIP FOR THE COMMON GOOD 70

CHAPTER 12: ECONOMIC EMPOWERMENT AND DEVELOPMENT 76

CHAPTER 13: EDUCATION AS A CATALYST FOR CHANGE 82

CHAPTER 14: BUILDING TRUST AND ACCOUNTABILITY 87

CHAPTER 15: PROMOTING MENTAL HEALTH AND WELL-BEING 93

CHAPTER 16: NAVIGATING CULTURAL SENSITIVITIES 98

CHAPTER 17: TRANSFORMATIVE JUSTICE AND RECONCILIATION 103

CHAPTER 18: REVOLUTIONIZING SOUTH AFRICA THROUGH INNOVATION AND CREATIVITY 108

CHAPTER 19: SUSTAINING COMMUNITY ENGAGEMENT 114

CHAPTER 20: A CALL TO UNMUTE COURAGEOUS CATALYSTS 120

Chapter 1: Understanding the Context

"To ignite true transformation, we must first confront the stark reality of our past and present with relentless honesty. South Africa's journey from the shadows of historical trauma and fragmentation to a future of unity and justice demands an unwavering commitment to understanding our context with radical clarity. This chapter is not just an introduction but a clarion call to recognize the deep-seated issues that bind us and to unmute our courageous catalysts for change."

The Unyielding Legacy of Historical Trauma

South Africa's history is a potent testament to the ravages of apartheid and colonialism. The apartheid regime's brutal imposition of racial segregation and economic disenfranchisement left scars that transcend time. The deliberate dismantling of community structures and the suppression of aspirations were not mere strategies but instruments of systemic oppression. These historical injustices continue to echo in our current socio-economic and cultural landscape.

Born in the rural village of KwaShange in the Inadi Tribal Authority in Pietermaritzburg, I grew up straddling vastly different worlds—the township of Umlazi in Durban and the opulence of Athlone Suburb in Pietermaritzburg. My formative years were spent navigating these extreme contrasts—between the tranquillity of a rural homestead, the volatility of Umlazi township, and the relative privilege of Athlone suburb. These disparate environments were more than just geographic locations; they were stark symbols of the systemic inequalities perpetuated by apartheid. Witnessing my family's daily struggles, particularly the harsh contradictions faced by those in my community, provided a profound education in the realities of historical trauma.

One vivid memory that encapsulates this contrast was a night when my mother took my cousin and me to an evening service at a beautiful church in Athlone. As we settled in, the pastor noticed us sitting at the back and kindly urged my mother to move forward, as if to erase any sense of being outsiders. We moved to the middle of the church, but the gesture was met with subtle rejection as a few families shifted sideways, creating a noticeable space between us and them. As a young boy, I was puzzled and hurt, wondering if there was something about us that made us unwelcome in a place where equality and unity should reign, worshipping the same God who promises us eternity together.

These early experiences of exclusion and disparity were not just about different places—they were emblematic of a broader system of injustice. The contrasts I witnessed were daily reminders of the deep-rooted inequities in our society.

These experiences instilled in me a profound understanding of the painful legacy of apartheid and the ongoing struggle against systemic inequality.

Reflecting on these realities, I am reminded of the Bible verse in Micah 6:8, which calls us to "act justly and to love mercy and to walk humbly with your God." This scripture serves as a guiding light, urging us to confront injustice with courage and to work tirelessly towards a just and reconciled society. The call to action is clear: we must address these systemic issues with integrity and boldness, acknowledging the historical context that continues to shape our present.

The Persistent Reality of Economic Inequality

Economic inequality is not merely a byproduct of historical injustices but a systemic issue deeply embedded in South Africa's socio-economic fabric. Despite the end of apartheid, the economic divide has not only persisted but has often widened. The continued accumulation of wealth and power by a privileged few while the majority languish in poverty reflects a profound failure to achieve equitable economic justice.

In my capacity as a social engagement facilitator and development practitioner, I have witnessed the devastating effects of economic inequality on communities. The lack of access to education, capital, and employment opportunities perpetuates cycles of poverty and exclusion. This economic injustice is a continuation of apartheid's legacy and requires a radical overhaul of our economic models. We need transformative policies that address root causes and ensure fair distribution of resources.

Mariana Mazzucato's assertion that "The economy should serve society, not the other way around" resonates deeply with me. This radical perspective emphasizes the need for systemic change that prioritizes equity and inclusive growth. Our approach must move beyond temporary fixes to implementing strategies that foster long-term, sustainable economic empowerment for all.

The Erosion of Social Cohesion and Volatility

Social cohesion in South Africa is under severe strain, marked by volatility and unrest. The scars of apartheid and ongoing socio-economic disparities manifest in explosive ways: from service delivery protests that disrupt communities to workplace tensions that fuel racial discord. The very fabric of our society is fraying under the pressure of these deep-seated issues.

The July 2021 KZN riots, which erupted during the legal battle between former President Jacob Zuma and the Constitutional Court, leading to his unprecedented arrest for contempt of court, were a stark manifestation of this volatility. The mass looting, destruction, and loss of over 300 lives were not isolated incidents but symptoms of a broader crisis. The mob mentality that took hold during these riots is a grim reminder of how quickly frustration and anger can escalate into widespread chaos. The ease with which people can be triggered into violence—whether in the name of race, culture, or perceived grievance—illustrates a dangerous disconnect from both rational discourse and communal empathy.

This volatility is compounded by high levels of substance abuse and a pervasive sense of hopelessness among the youth. The rampant use of drugs and alcohol among young South Africans is not just a personal failing but a societal issue, deeply rooted in systemic neglect and disenfranchisement. The loss of hope and direction is a clear indicator of a failed system that has not provided adequate support or opportunities for our younger generation.

Moreover, the division within our faith communities underscores the fractured nature of our national identity. Churches and other religious entities are often divided along racial lines, reflecting broader societal divisions. This fragmentation of faith communities further exacerbates social tensions and undermines collective efforts towards reconciliation and unity.

The Legacy of Bantustans and Tribal Divisions

The imposition of Bantustans during apartheid was a calculated strategy to fragment and control Black South Africans. These pseudo-national homelands were designed for the country's Black African population, broken down into linguistic and tribal domains. These were rooted in Land Acts promulgated in 1913 and 1936, which defined several scattered areas as "native reserves" for Blacks. By creating artificial tribal boundaries and instituting a system of black-on-black violence, apartheid deepened tribal divisions and perpetuated conflict within marginalized communities. This sowing of discord has had a lasting impact, manifesting in persistent tribalism and stereotyping that continues to plague our society.

The divisions created by the Bantustans are not just historical footnotes but active issues today. The tribal stereotypes and prejudices that emerged have left deep wounds and fostered a culture of exploitation and division. Instead of working towards reconciliation, many communities have succumbed to intra-racial tensions and exploitation. The historical manipulation of tribal identities has given rise to harmful stereotypes and discrimination that perpetuate division and hinder collective progress.

This fragmentation is further exacerbated by the stigmatization along tribal and racial lines. In some instances, religious denominational differences contribute to the division, as different faith groups become sources of conflict rather than unity. The exploitation within previously marginalized communities, where individuals and groups prioritize self-interest over collective healing, only deepens the crisis.

The Crisis of White Supremacy and the Quest for Assimilation

The lingering influence of white supremacy manifests in various ways, including the pernicious belief that whiteness is synonymous with excellence and affluence. This deeply ingrained mindset continues to affect societal norms and aspirations, creating a toxic environment where assimilation to perceived standards of whiteness is seen as a pathway to success.

In some circles, the quest for assimilation reflects a broader failure to embrace and celebrate diversity. The perpetuation of white-centric standards undermines the value of authentic cultural identities and reinforces existing inequalities. This dynamic perpetuates a cycle of privilege and exclusion, where those who do not conform to these standards are marginalized and disadvantaged.

The manifestation of privilege, where access to opportunities is based on historical advantage and proximity to whiteness, further exacerbates societal divisions. The disparity in access and opportunity highlights the urgent need for a radical rethinking of our systems and structures to ensure genuine equity and inclusion.

The Crisis of Leadership and Governance

The state of South African leadership and governance is a reflection of the broader societal challenges we face. Corruption, inefficiency, and a lack of accountability have eroded public trust and perpetuated a cycle of disillusionment. Effective leadership must rise above mediocrity and embrace a vision rooted in integrity, transparency, and commitment to the common good.

As a political activist and development practitioner, I have seen the urgent need for radical reformation in leadership and governance. Leaders must not only articulate bold visions but also embody the principles of justice, equity, and service. This requires a departure from entrenched practices and a commitment to creating a culture of accountability and excellence.

Thuli Madonsela's perspective that "True leadership is not about power or position; it is about commitment to serving the people with integrity and excellence" aligns with my convictions. This radical vision of leadership challenges us to demand and embody new standards that prioritize the well-being of all citizens and foster effective governance.

Embracing Radical Reformation and Healing

Moving forward necessitates embracing radical reformation. This is not about incremental change but about a complete overhaul of systems that perpetuate inequality and division. Understanding our context is the first step in this transformative process. It requires confronting uncomfortable truths, rejecting superficial solutions, and adopting bold, innovative approaches.

Healing from historical trauma involves concrete action, not just acknowledgment. We must address the root causes of socio-economic and cultural challenges with comprehensive, systemic approaches. This includes advocating for policy reforms, investing in community-led development, and fostering a culture of inclusivity and justice.

Every South African has a role in this transformation. Whether you are an activist, a policymaker, an educator, or an ordinary citizen, you are called to be a catalyst for change. Our nation's future depends on our collective ability to confront our past, challenge our present, and work towards a future of justice and unity.

"The time for passive observation has ended. The future of South Africa demands an active, courageous response from every one of us. Our journey towards a unified, equitable nation requires radical action and a steadfast commitment to confronting and overcoming our historical and present-day challenges."

This call to action is not merely an invitation but a demand for radical participation. The courageous catalysts—those who dare to challenge the status quo and envision a future of justice and unity—are the ones who will lead South Africa beyond its historical trauma and fragmentation. As we embark on this journey, let us commit to a path of transformative change, guided by the unwavering principles of justice, equity, and reconciliation.

Chapter 2: Cultivating Empathy and Compassion

In the heart of South Africa's transformative journey towards healing, empathy and compassion are not just virtues—they are revolutionary forces. As a nation deeply scarred by the legacy of apartheid and colonial oppression, we confront the reality of unresolved trauma that pervades our communities, institutions, and relationships. This chapter is a bold call to action for us to embrace empathy and compassion with unyielding fervor and to act as courageous catalysts in the face of these enduring challenges.

Contextualizing Empathy and Compassion

Empathy transcends mere recognition of others' emotions; it demands that we immerse ourselves in their experiences and feel their pain as our own. Compassion takes this understanding and drives us to act, seeking to alleviate suffering with relentless dedication. In a society still reeling from historical injustices, these principles are not optional—they are essential for true healing and progress. We must engage deeply and transform the narrative of pain into a collective journey of upliftment and solidarity.

Historical Context and Trauma

The indelible marks of apartheid and colonial rule continue to shape our society, manifesting in systemic inequalities, deteriorating work standards, and waning patriotism. These issues are not isolated but are deeply rooted in the unresolved traumas of our past. As leaders and professionals, many of us grapple with our own wounds—some have reaped the benefits of past inequities, while others bear the scars of injustice. This disparity undermines effective leadership and fosters fragmentation across our educational institutions, workplaces, and public services.

The lack of empathy and declining work quality reveal deeper systemic problems. Unresolved trauma within leadership circles often translates into broader societal dysfunctions—where trust is fractured, patriotism is diluted, and quality of life remains uneven. Addressing these traumas is not merely about personal healing; it is about forging a collective path toward societal advancement. As we confront these wounds with radical empathy and unyielding compassion, we lay the groundwork for a unified, equitable South Africa.

Personal Journey and Lessons

From the age of six, I began to understand the impact of compassion and empathy through observing my mother, who, despite having me as her only child and not earning much income, supported over ten others in both related to our family and just ordinary community people. This early exposure to selflessness taught me the values of sharing and justice. At that young age, I also started standing up for those being bullied or mistreated, a legacy that continued through my teenage years. I engaged in various resistance campaigns and faced conflicts with authorities in school, church, sports, and other areas, all while advocating for fairness and inclusion.

This journey of empathy led me to student politics and Christian leadership, where I sought to balance governance and spirituality as key drivers of compassion and justice. In my professional life, this commitment extended to becoming a labor representative, advocating for employees' rights, and later, as a business owner, hiring individuals with challenging personal histories. This consistent dedication to empathy and compassion has profoundly shaped my approach to leadership and community engagement, transforming both my professional and personal interactions

Biblical Foundations for Empathy and Compassion

The teachings of Jesus Christ offer a radical framework for empathy and compassion that transcends religious boundaries and speaks to our shared humanity:

- **Matthew 25:35-40:** Jesus highlights that serving those who are marginalized and oppressed is a profound expression of our spiritual commitment. Acts of kindness toward the needy are not just charitable; they are fundamental to our shared humanity and justice. This teaching compels us to engage deeply with those who suffer and to address their needs with urgency and sincerity.
- **Luke 10:25-37:** The parable of the Good Samaritan challenges us to extend compassion beyond societal and personal biases. It calls us to assist those in need, irrespective of their background or our own prejudices. This story underscores the importance of engaging with others' pain meaningfully and non-judgmentally, fostering a culture of empathy and support.

These Biblical principles demand that we lead with empathy and compassion, aligning ourselves with a path of understanding and transformative action. They call us to move beyond superficial engagement and commit to profound, actionable change.

Practical Approaches to Cultivating Empathy and Compassion

To cultivate genuine empathy, we must immerse ourselves in the diverse experiences of others:

- **Active Listening:** This requires more than surface-level conversation; it demands that we engage fully, absorbing and understanding the perspectives and challenges of people from various backgrounds. My experience in facilitating dialogues with students, leaders, and community members has

shown that active listening builds profound connections and fosters a deeper understanding of others' realities. It is through these meaningful interactions that we bridge gaps and cultivate true empathy.
- **Immersive Engagement:** Participating in community events and interacting with people from different social settings provide critical insights. My involvement with communities in Umlazi, Isipingo, and Durban Central has highlighted the importance of understanding the complexities of various social issues. By engaging directly with these communities, we gain a comprehensive understanding of their challenges and build solidarity across diverse contexts.

Educational Initiatives

Educational programs are essential in nurturing empathy and compassion:
- **Curriculum Development:** Integrating the history of apartheid and its effects into educational content helps build a shared understanding of our socio-economic challenges. By embedding this historical perspective, we promote empathy and encourage collective action towards meaningful change. This approach has been instrumental in various workshops and training sessions I have conducted, fostering a deeper understanding of our shared history and its impact on current issues.
- **Workshops and Training:** Organizing workshops on themes like "Healing Historical Wounds," "Building Bridges Across Cultures," and "Empowering Youth Through Understanding" facilitates significant dialogue. Interactive elements such as role-playing, and group discussions enhance engagement with empathy and compassion. These workshops are designed to drive deep, transformative conversations, addressing deep-seated issues and fostering understanding.

Compassionate Leadership Models

Leaders must embody empathy and compassion through deliberate and impactful strategies:
- **Inclusive Decision-Making:** Leaders must include diverse voices in decision-making processes to promote equity and foster trust. By ensuring decisions reflect a wide range of perspectives, we address systemic biases and reinforce a sense of shared purpose. My experience facilitating elections and strategic planning workshops has demonstrated the importance of inclusive decision-making in fostering trust and achieving effective outcomes.
- **Supportive Mentoring:** Establishing mentorship programs focused on holistic development is crucial. Compassionate mentoring supports emerging leaders by building their confidence, resilience, and skills. Tailoring mentorship to address the specific needs of individuals from various backgrounds enhances their ability to navigate challenges effectively.
- **Community-Based Solutions:** Developing solutions in collaboration with communities ensures that initiatives address the root causes of social issues.

Engaging community members in planning and implementation fosters ownership and ensures that solutions are relevant and impactful. My work with local businesses, job seekers, and community organizations has shown that community-driven solutions are vital for addressing complex social issues.

Navigating Complex Contexts: Practical Insights

Navigating South Africa's multifaceted realities demands a nuanced application of empathy and compassion. My extensive experience across diverse settings offers critical insights:

- **Bridging Gaps in Diverse Communities:** Addressing poverty and high unemployment in Umlazi required a nuanced understanding of the community's struggles and aspirations. Initiatives had to provide practical support while fostering dignity and self-worth. In Isipingo, balancing cultural and socio-economic diversity involved integrating different expectations to promote inclusivity. In Durban Central, understanding the pressures faced by urban residents and creating platforms for mutual respect were essential for fostering collaboration.
- **Addressing Tensions and Conflicts:** Mediating conflicts between developers, local businesses, and job seekers underscored the need to address underlying grievances. Whether dealing with construction mafias or service delivery protests, empathy involved recognizing and addressing the root causes of tension. In student unrest, understanding both students' frustrations and institutional constraints was key to finding common ground and implementing effective solutions.
- **Facilitating Holistic Development:** As a community leader and pastor, fostering holistic development meant addressing immediate needs while nurturing long-term aspirations. In Umlazi, this involved implementing development initiatives to alleviate poverty. In more affluent areas, the focus shifted to promoting social cohesion and economic opportunity. Effective leadership requires a deep commitment to addressing both individual and collective needs.
- **Developing Inclusive Solutions:** Creating inclusive solutions involved engaging communities to ensure initiatives are relevant and impactful. This meant developing training programs, community forums, and economic development initiatives that reflected diverse needs. By fostering a culture of empathy and collaboration, we can address complex societal challenges effectively.
- **Empowering Local Leaders:** Investing in local leadership is crucial for addressing community-specific challenges. Providing training, support, and mentorship enhances emerging leaders' capacity to drive positive change. Empowering local leaders builds a culture of resilience and growth, ensuring that empathy and compassion are embedded in community development efforts.

Conclusion
Cultivating empathy and compassion is not a noble ideal but a radical necessity for effective leadership and societal transformation in South Africa. By confronting historical traumas, drawing on timeless principles of empathy and compassion, and implementing practical strategies, we can pave the way for a more inclusive and equitable society. Engaging with anti-racism efforts, addressing trauma, and rebuilding trust are essential steps in this journey.

Recognizing and addressing the personal struggles of leaders is vital for creating an environment where both leaders and communities can heal and thrive. As we strive to embody these values with unwavering commitment, we contribute to a more just and compassionate world, aligned with the principles that guide us toward deeper understanding and meaningful action.

Chapter 3: Developing Resilience in South Africa

Resilience is not merely an admirable trait; it is a radical, transformative force essential for the survival and prosperity of our communities. This chapter serves as a bold call to action, urging readers to embrace resilience not just as a concept but as a lived reality. It is a demand to confront our traumatic history with courage, commit to relentless action, and transform current challenges into opportunities for profound change.

Historical Context and Its Impact

South Africa's path to resilience is intricately tied to its troubled history. The oppressive legacy of apartheid and colonialism has left an indelible mark on society, manifesting in deep-seated socio-economic disparities and systemic dysfunction. This legacy isn't a relic of the past but a continuing force that shapes present struggles and demands a radical response.

The Scars of Apartheid and Colonial Exploitation

The historical injustices of apartheid and colonialism are not superficial blemishes but deep, systemic wounds that affect every aspect of society. These injustices have created a legacy of inequality and fragmentation that demands more than just acknowledgement; they require radical, transformative action. Efforts must go beyond surface-level reforms to address the root causes of these systemic issues.

Reflecting on my own experiences working in social engagement and community development, I have seen firsthand how these systemic issues continue to affect individuals and communities. It has become clear that addressing these wounds requires more than just policy changes; it requires a collective will to drive transformative action.

Confronting the Urgency

The discord and mistrust sown by these historical traumas have escalated to a critical point, where the urgency to confront these realities is dire. The call to action is clear: if not us, then who will rise to confront the challenges before us? Complaining and lamenting about the flaws and failures of the system will not lead to change. It is up to each of us to stand up and address the stubborn legacy of apartheid and colonialism, which continues to manifest in different layers across society.

Through my work, I've encountered countless individuals who embody this sense of urgency—those who refuse to be passive observers in the face of injustice. Their courage and commitment inspire the kind of resilience we need to cultivate across all levels of society.

Absent Fathers and Broken Family Units

The absence of fathers and the fragmentation of family units are not just social issues but are deeply intertwined with the history of systemic oppression. These broken family structures perpetuate instability, undermine community cohesion, and contribute to ongoing cycles of poverty and dysfunction. Addressing these issues requires a radical rethinking of how families are supported and empowered, making it a cornerstone of building resilience.

In my engagements with communities, I've often seen the devastating effects of these broken structures. Programs that focus on family support and mentorship have proven effective in rebuilding the foundations necessary for resilience, but these efforts must be scaled and sustained.

Strengthening National Identity and Patriotism

The erosion of national identity and patriotism has weakened collective resolve and unity. The fragmentation of national identity hampers the ability to build a cohesive society and work towards common goals. Reconstructing national identity is not just about pride; it's about fostering a sense of shared purpose and unity, essential for driving resilience and fostering a united front against the challenges faced by the nation.

In community-building projects that I've been involved in, promoting cultural heritage and national dialogue has been a central theme. These efforts are crucial in restoring a collective identity that can serve as the bedrock for resilience.

Engaging and Empowering Youth

Engaging youth in constructive activities is a key strategy in combating reckless behaviors that often stem from systemic neglect. Providing opportunities for skill development, mentorship, and community involvement not only redirects energy but also fosters resilience and drives meaningful change. The youth, empowered and skilled, become vital agents of transformation in their communities.

I've seen the power of youth engagement firsthand. Whether through leadership workshops or community service projects, young people have the potential to lead the charge in building a resilient society. Their energy and vision are indispensable in this effort.

Resilience Through Consistent Effort

Developing resilience is not about merely enduring difficulties but about committing to consistent, transformative action. It's about working tirelessly, often in the face of adversity, driven by the belief that every effort contributes to long-term progress. Resilience is the result of sustained effort and dedication, even when the results are not immediately visible.

In my role as a facilitator and mediator, I've learned that resilience often comes from the persistent, behind-the-scenes work that slowly but surely builds a foundation for lasting change. It's this kind of steady, unwavering commitment that we need to nurture in our communities.

Ethical Integrity

Resilience also involves standing firm against ethical erosion and systemic corruption. Maintaining high ethical standards in challenging environments requires unwavering commitment and courage. Resilience, therefore, is not just about weathering external challenges but also about upholding internal principles, which are crucial for driving systemic change.

Throughout my career, I've encountered situations that tested my ethical boundaries. Standing firm in these moments has not only reinforced my own resilience but has also inspired others to do the same, creating ripples of integrity that strengthen our collective resolve.

Confronting Deep-Seated Wounds

Addressing deep-seated wounds requires a comprehensive, systemic approach. Superficial solutions are insufficient for dealing with the root causes of societal problems. True resilience demands tackling these issues at their core, with sensitivity and care, and with a commitment to lasting solutions.

Transforming Reckless Behaviors

Reckless behaviors often reflect deeper societal issues rooted in historical trauma and systemic dysfunction. Addressing these behaviors requires a radical approach that goes beyond surface-level interventions. It involves understanding the underlying causes of these behaviors and implementing transformative solutions that address these root issues.

Trauma-Informed Practices

Recognizing and addressing the impact of historical trauma is essential for genuine healing. Trauma-informed practices, which focus on understanding and addressing underlying pain, are crucial for developing effective strategies to heal and empower individuals and communities. Implementing these practices at the community level is vital, creating safe spaces for dialogue and fostering resilience.

In my work with trauma recovery programs, I've seen the profound difference that trauma-informed approaches can make. These practices not only help individuals heal but also empower them to become resilient leaders in their communities.

Community Empowerment

Empowering communities to drive their own progress is crucial for building resilience. Participatory development and community-led projects foster a sense of agency and ownership, transforming communities into powerful agents of change. Successful community-driven projects demonstrate the potential for resilience when communities are empowered to lead their own development.

Having supported various community-led initiatives, I can attest to the transformative power of empowerment. When people feel they have a stake in their own progress, they become more resilient and capable of overcoming the challenges they face.

Fostering Personal Resilience

Personal resilience is equally critical. Prioritizing self-care, mental health, and skill development is fundamental for individuals to navigate challenges and contribute to societal resilience. Programs that focus on personal development help individuals build the strength and confidence needed to face challenges and contribute to a more resilient society.

In my personal journey, I've learned that resilience begins with self-care and personal growth. It's a lesson I've tried to pass on through workshops and mentoring, knowing that resilient individuals are the foundation of resilient communities.

Policy and Institutional Support

Sustainable resilience requires supportive policies and institutional frameworks. Inclusive policies that address historical injustices and promote equity are essential for creating a foundation of resilience. Policies that promote social and economic equity have had transformative impacts, highlighting the importance of inclusive policy development in fostering resilience.

Investing in Infrastructure

Investing in infrastructure that supports community well-being and economic stability is essential for resilience. Community centers, emergency response systems, and economic development projects create a solid foundation for community well-being and stability, mitigating the impacts of disruptions and facilitating recovery.

Rebuilding Trust and Bridging Gaps

Building resilience involves bridging the gap between communities and institutions. Rebuilding trust through transparency, accountability, and consistent engagement is essential for effective collaboration. Joint efforts between government, civil society, and the private sector have shown significant success in tackling complex issues, underscoring the importance of effective collaboration in building resilience.

The Story of the Four Lepers: A Model of Radical Resilience

The story of the four leprous men from 2 Kings 7 offers a powerful lesson in radical resilience. Facing a devastating famine and siege, these men confronted a stark choice: remain in their dire situation or take a bold risk by moving forward into the unknown. Their decision to act was not merely about survival; it was a radical, transformative act that changed their entire community's fate.

A Defining Moment of Courage

In the face of overwhelming odds, the lepers chose to act with courage and determination. They asked, "Why stay here until we die?" Their decision to advance, despite the risks, was an act of defiance against a hopeless status quo. This story serves as a profound metaphor for our current situation in South

Africa. It's a call to move beyond inertia, to confront challenges with radical courage, and to take decisive action towards transformation.

Embracing Change and Moving Forward

The lepers' decision led to the discovery of abundant resources, transforming their dire situation into one of hope and prosperity. This transformation underscores the power of radical resilience. By embracing change and acting with courage, current challenges can be turned into opportunities for growth and prosperity.

Call to Action

In light of this story, we are all called to embrace our own moments of courage and transformation. We must confront our challenges head-on, take bold actions, and work together to create a future of resilience and prosperity. The ability to effect change depends on a collective willingness to act decisively and courageously, even when the path forward is uncertain.

Conclusion

Developing resilience in South Africa is a radical, transformative process that requires a deep, systemic approach. It involves confronting historical traumas, committing to consistent effort, and embracing personal and collective courage. By drawing on these experiences, the lessons from the story of the four lepers, and a commitment to justice and equity, a resilient society capable of overcoming the most pressing challenges and forging a brighter future can be built.

As we move forward, let us remember that resilience is not merely about surviving but thriving in the face of adversity. It is about transforming challenges into opportunities for profound change. Together, we can unmute our courageous voices and lead South Africa beyond its historical traumas towards a future of hope, unity, and resilience.

Chapter 4: Effective Communication

In South Africa, effective communication is not merely a skill; it is a radical and transformative lifeline for unity, healing, and progress. It serves as the mechanism through which we bridge divides, foster understanding, and drive change that shakes the very foundations of a fragmented society. Communication is the weapon with which we combat the pervasive remnants of our painful history, and it is the heartbeat of unmuting courageous catalysts—those who challenge the status quo, envision a better future and inspire others to rise and act.

Lessons from Revolutionary Communicators

History is replete with leaders who used communication as a powerful tool to mobilize people under the most daunting conditions. Nelson Mandela, for instance, didn't just speak to the people; he spoke with them, articulating a vision of reconciliation and unity amidst the divisive aftermath of apartheid. His words were not just rhetoric; they were a rallying cry that galvanized a nation towards collective healing and transformation. Similarly, Martin Luther King Jr. didn't merely dream of justice; he communicated that dream with such eloquence that it transcended barriers and inspired millions to join the struggle for civil rights. But let's not forget those like Steve Biko, who communicated a radical, unflinching vision of Black Consciousness that empowered a generation to rise up against oppression. Biko's words were so powerful that they were seen as a threat to the apartheid regime, leading to his silencing by the state. This is the power of communication—it can transcend adversity, rally people around a common purpose, and drive profound societal shifts, even in the face of brutal opposition.

Personal Experience with Communication

Growing up in South Africa, I learned the hard way that communication can be both a bridge and a weapon. At a boys' camp near Umnini Beach in 1992, my innocent attempt to greet Afrikaner fishermen in Afrikaans resulted in a harsh slap—a painful reminder of how easily communication can be misinterpreted and escalate into conflict. This incident, along with others, taught me that our words and gestures must be handled with the utmost care and precision. Miscommunication is not just a misstep; it can be a catalyst for violence and destruction.

In my neighborhood, miscommunication often had catastrophic consequences—homes were burned, families shattered, and lives irreparably damaged. At the age of ten, I was brutally punished for a private conversation that was misquoted, and I witnessed a family narrowly avoid disaster after being falsely accused of stockpiling weapons for political violence. These experiences underscore the immense power of communication—how it can either destroy or build, tear apart or bring together.

In higher education, the communication crisis is nothing short of a scandal. The tensions between management and student leaders are often exacerbated by a severe breakdown in communication. Instead of engaging in genuine, transparent dialogue, both sides have allowed egos, titles, and entrenched positions to create barriers that deepen mistrust and frustration. This isn't just a minor issue—it's a systemic failure that perpetuates conflict and hinders progress. We must radically overhaul how institutions approach communication, emphasizing clarity, empathy, and active listening to resolve disputes and foster a more collaborative environment.

Communication as a Tool for Liberation

In South Africa, communication is not just a means to an end; it is a tool for liberation. Through dialogue, we confront our past, challenge the present, and lay the groundwork for a more equitable future. Effective communication articulates grievances, shares stories of struggle, and mobilizes communities towards collective action. It creates channels for open dialogue, allowing marginalized voices to be heard and explored, and solutions that are inclusive and just. By dismantling systemic barriers and fostering a shared sense of purpose, communication becomes the means by which we break free from the chains of our history.

And yet, let's be clear—communication is not just about words. It's about action. It's about wielding our voices as weapons in the fight for justice. Silence is complicity. If we do not speak out, if we do not confront the forces that seek to divide and oppress us, then we have chosen the side of the oppressor.

Channels for Healing and Restoration

Communication is essential for healing and restoration. It involves creating spaces where individuals and communities can express their experiences, confront their traumas, and work towards reconciliation. In a country where historical and ongoing wounds continue to fester, communication plays a key role in the healing process. Establishing channels for dialogue that emerge from grassroots and informal processes is crucial. These channels facilitate community conversations, healing workshops, and restorative justice initiatives—each serving to acknowledge past harms, provide support, and address the root causes of conflict.

But let's not mistake communication for mere conversation. It is an active, relentless pursuit of truth and reconciliation. It is about demanding that the wounds of the past be acknowledged, that justice be served, and that the voices of the oppressed be amplified, not just heard.

Building Trust Through Transparent Communication

Building trust through transparent communication is another vital aspect. Transparency is not a luxury; it is a necessity for rebuilding trust and fostering collaboration. By being open about intentions, decisions, and processes, we address skepticism and create a foundation for mutual understanding. However, effective communication requires more than just openness—it demands a radical commitment to overcoming various barriers, including cultural sensitivities, historical context, and emotional dynamics. Understanding and respecting cultural differences in communication styles ensures interactions are respectful and inclusive. Acknowledging the historical backdrop helps address issues with empathy and understanding, while managing emotional responses prevents escalation and maintains a constructive dialogue.

In this age, where misinformation spreads like wildfire and trust in institutions is eroded, transparency is revolutionary. It is an act of defiance against a system that thrives on secrecy and deception. By demanding and practicing transparency, we challenge the very structures that have long kept us divided and disempowered.

Investing in Communication Skills

To wield communication as a tool for radical change, we must invest in the skills that make it effective. Training and workshops provide opportunities for individuals to develop essential skills such as active listening, clarity in messaging, and conflict resolution. Mentorship and coaching offer the guidance needed to refine these skills, while feedback mechanisms help to identify and address communication gaps. This investment is not just about improving interaction; it's about equipping leaders and communities with the tools needed to drive transformation.

This is not just about speaking well—it's about speaking powerfully. It's about crafting messages that cut through the noise, that challenge assumptions, that provoke action. It's about preparing ourselves and our communities to be not just participants in dialogue but leaders in the fight for change.

Leading with Communication

Leaders play a critical role in modeling and promoting effective communication. By exemplifying best practices, fostering open dialogue, and addressing issues head-on, leaders set the standard for others and build credibility. But leading with communication goes beyond polite discourse—it requires speaking truthfully and boldly, empathizing deeply, and inspiring others towards collective goals. Courageous communication involves confronting uncomfortable truths, proposing bold solutions, and articulating the pain and aspirations of the people. It is through such communication that leaders can mobilize action and drive meaningful change.

Leadership is not about holding a title—it's about holding the truth. And in South Africa, where our history is marred by lies and deceit, the truth is revolutionary. Leaders must not only speak the truth but must do so with the courage and clarity that inspire others to join the fight for justice.

The Heart of Unmuting Courageous Catalysts

Communication is the heartbeat of unmuting courageous catalysts—those individuals who dare to challenge the status quo, envision a better future, and inspire others to follow. In our quest to address South Africa's deep-seated challenges, it is imperative that we cultivate a form of communication that does more than inform—it must ignite action. The art of unmuting courageous catalysts demands a profound commitment to truth, empathy, and transformation. It requires leaders to speak with conviction, to listen with compassion, and to act with decisiveness.

Biblical Insight: The Power of Words

The Bible offers profound wisdom on the power of words. Proverbs 18:21 states, "The tongue has the power of life and death, and those who love it will eat its fruit." This scripture highlights the immense impact that words can have—they can build up or tear down, heal or hurt. In the context of South Africa's challenges, effective communication must be used to foster life, encourage healing, and drive positive change. It is a responsibility that we cannot take lightly.

But let us also remember that the words we speak in the face of injustice are not just for healing—they are for liberation. They are for breaking the chains of oppression, for tearing down the walls of division, for building a future where truth and justice reign.

Call to Action

As we conclude this exploration of effective communication, it is clear that our words and actions hold transformative power. But this power is wasted if it is not used to challenge, to provoke, to inspire. We must use communication as a tool to drive progress, heal wounds, and build trust. It is time to transition from understanding communication principles to actively leading with courage.

So, I challenge you—are you ready to speak the truth? Are you ready to use your voice as a weapon in the fight for justice? Are you prepared to confront the lies that have held us back and to build a future rooted in truth, empathy, and action?

In the next chapter, we will dive into the essence of leading with courage. We will explore how to confront challenges boldly, inspire others, and act decisively in the face of adversity. Courageous leadership is not just about making tough decisions but also about fostering a culture of bravery and resilience. Join me as we uncover the practices and principles that define courageous leadership and set the stage for unmuting the catalysts who will drive South Africa towards a more hopeful and united future.

Chapter 5: Leading with Courage

Leading with courage is not merely an aspect of effective leadership; it is the core of transformative leadership that has the power to reshape lives, challenge oppressive systems, and redefine futures. Courageous leadership involves standing firm on one's principles, confronting challenges head-on, and making decisions that serve the greater good despite personal risk. It requires an unyielding commitment to values and a vision that extends beyond immediate obstacles. True leaders who exhibit courage are not deterred by potential fallout; instead, they are driven by an unwavering resolve and integrity, guided by a higher purpose and an enduring vision of justice.

Historical Pillars of Courageous Leadership

Throughout history, certain leaders have embodied the essence of courageous leadership, facing immense challenges to drive change and justice. In South Africa, Albertina Sisulu stands as a beacon of courageous leadership. Her unwavering commitment to equality and justice during the apartheid era, despite severe personal risk, highlights the essence of true bravery. Sisulu's role in galvanizing grassroots support against apartheid is a testament to her profound impact on the struggle for justice.

Chris Hani's leadership in the South African Communist Party and Umkhonto we Sizwe also serves as a powerful example of courage. Hani's dedication to resisting apartheid and his vision for a democratic South Africa were crucial in mobilizing support and inspiring hope among the oppressed, demonstrating the strength of leadership driven by conviction.

Winnie Madikizela-Mandela, known as the "Mother of the Nation," displayed remarkable courage in her relentless fight against apartheid. Her resilience and commitment to the marginalized, despite personal sacrifices and political challenges, made her a powerful symbol of resistance and hope for many. Her courage wasn't just in her defiance of the apartheid regime but in her willingness to stand up to those who sought to silence her within her own ranks.

Nicholas Bengu, an influential apostolic leader and founder of the Africa Back to God Crusades in the 1950s in South Africa, reflects a different dimension of courageous leadership. His efforts in advancing Kingdom principles and addressing societal issues through various community-building campaigns exposed his bravery in confronting systemic challenges and advocating for spiritual and social renewal.

These leaders did not just lead—they rebelled. They stood against the tides of oppression, challenging not only the external forces of apartheid but also the internal divisions and betrayals within their own movements. Their courage was radical, uncompromising, and deeply transformative.

Courage in the Broader African Context

Across the African continent, leaders such as Kwame Nkrumah of Ghana have demonstrated exemplary courage. Nkrumah's bold pursuit of African independence and his leadership in the Pan-African movement were marked by transformative policies that reshaped the post-colonial African landscape.

Patrice Lumumba, the first Prime Minister of the Democratic Republic of Congo, exhibited incredible bravery in his fight for Congolese sovereignty. His dedication to social justice, despite facing intense opposition and ultimately paying the ultimate price, highlights his unwavering commitment to his people's freedom and dignity. Lumumba's courage wasn't just in his defiance of colonial powers but in his refusal to bend to the internal pressures that sought to undermine his vision for a truly independent Congo.

Jomo Kenyatta's leadership as Kenya's first President was characterized by his courage in uniting a diverse nation and guiding it toward independence. Kenyatta's negotiations with colonial powers and his focus on nation-building were pivotal in Kenya's transition from colonial rule to self-governance. But his leadership also faced criticism, and the courage he exhibited in navigating those complexities highlights the multifaceted nature of true leadership.

These African leaders were not just figureheads—they were warriors, battling not just the external forces of colonialism but the internal challenges of leading diverse, often divided nations towards a unified future.

The Foundations of Courageous Leadership

Courageous leadership is built on several fundamental attributes. At its core, it involves maintaining steadfast adherence to one's values and principles, even when faced with significant challenges. Leaders who embody courage are driven by a vision that transcends immediate obstacles, willing to confront difficult truths, and make decisions that are aligned with their core beliefs.

Resilience is another critical component of courageous leadership. It requires the ability to endure setbacks, face criticism, and persist through adversity. This resilience is not merely about withstanding challenges but about learning and growing from them. Courageous leaders view failure as an opportunity for growth, refining their strategies and approaches based on their experiences.

Empathy is also essential for courageous leadership. Leaders must be attuned to the human aspect of their decisions and actions. They need to listen to the concerns and aspirations of those they lead and make choices that benefit their people, even if it involves personal discomfort or risk.

But let's be clear—courageous leadership is not for the faint-hearted. It's not about making popular decisions or avoiding conflict. It's about standing in the fire, confronting the uncomfortable, and pushing through fear to do what is right, not what is easy.

Confronting South Africa's Adversities with Courage

South Africa's historical and contemporary challenges underscore the necessity of courageous leadership. The legacy of apartheid, ongoing socio-economic disparities, and community volatility demand leaders who are not only visionary but also bold in addressing these issues directly.

In 2011, I was called to lead a political tolerance intervention at Mangosuthu University of Technology (MUT), where the student body was deeply divided. The tensions between SADESMO (IFP-affiliated) and NASMO (NFP-affiliated) had reached a boiling point, with both sides fiercely locked in conflict. Their traditional rivals, SASCO and other PYA components such as ANCYL and YCLSA, were momentarily catching a small break amidst the heightened tensions between SADESMO and NASMO. However, the situation was volatile enough that even these rivals were indirectly drawn into the chaos, and external stakeholders began manipulating the tensions for their own political gains.

Leading that process required deep courage. The environment was charged with aggression, and the risks were significant. I had to bring together all the leaders involved, calling them to order and creating a space where they could trust the process I was facilitating. This wasn't just about mediating a truce—it was about encouraging these leaders to have the courage to manage their own organizations while working together to confront the crisis and tensions head-on. Through persistent dialogue and fostering mutual understanding, all stakeholders eventually worked together to confront the crisis and restore stability.

Many years later, as a social engagement practitioner and mediator, I have seen the fruits of courageous leadership manifest not only in my actions but also in the actions of my team members and those we served at that critical time. This experience taught me that courageous leadership is about facing the toughest challenges with integrity and guiding others to do the same.

Another profound example of courageous leadership emerged during the COVID-19 pandemic and subsequent lockdowns. Faith leaders and organizations in KwaZulu-Natal (KZN) came together under the banner of Local Ecumenical Action Networks (LEANs). In the face of a global crisis that brought fear, uncertainty, and widespread suffering, these leaders demonstrated remarkable courage. Various specialist organizations assigned resources and skills to serve the people of KZN, both within the church and in the broader community. They did not wait for instructions or support from the state; instead, they mobilized quickly, responding to the urgent needs of the people. This collective action was not just a response to a crisis—it was a demonstration of faith in action, of leadership that puts the well-being of others at the forefront, even in the most challenging of times.

The absence of fathers, broken family units, lack of national identity and patriotism, and the prevalence of reckless lifestyles are manifestations of deeper societal wounds. Courageous leaders must confront these issues with honesty and a commitment to transformative, long-term solutions. Addressing these systemic problems requires more than temporary fixes; it demands a comprehensive engagement with the root causes of these challenges.

Leading through adversity involves facing uncomfortable truths and engaging with them directly. Courageous leaders must address systemic injustices, advocate for equitable policies, and foster environments that promote healing and growth. They need to challenge entrenched norms and practices that perpetuate inequality and division.

This is not about patching up the cracks—it's about tearing down the walls of injustice and rebuilding a society on the foundations of truth, equity, and justice. Courageous leadership in South Africa means standing up to the deeply ingrained systems of oppression that still linger and pushing forward with radical reforms that shake the very core of our societal structures.

Building a Culture of Courage

Creating a culture that supports courageous leadership involves encouraging and celebrating bravery. It requires providing leaders with the support and resources needed to make bold decisions and take decisive actions. Training programs, mentorship, and peer support are vital in helping leaders develop the confidence and skills necessary for courageous action.

But building a culture of courage goes beyond mere support—it demands a collective commitment to challenge mediocrity and complacency. It requires a community willing to hold its leaders accountable, to push them towards greater integrity and action, and to celebrate those who take the hard road of truth and justice.

It is also important to create spaces for open dialogue and reflection. Leaders need opportunities to discuss their challenges, share their experiences, and seek advice from others who have navigated similar situations. By fostering networks of support and learning, we can enhance the capacity for courageous action and inspire others to embrace bravery in their own leadership roles.

A culture of courage is one where fear is not the driving force—where the fear of failure, the fear of backlash, the fear of standing alone is overshadowed by the commitment to justice and truth.

Faith and Values as Sources of Courage

For those guided by faith, the principles of courage are deeply rooted in spiritual teachings. Biblical narratives offer profound examples of courageous leadership. Joshua 1:9 states, "Have

I not commanded you? Be strong and courageous. Do not be afraid; do not be discouraged, for the Lord your God will be with you wherever you go." This verse encapsulates the essence of courageous leadership—trusting in a higher purpose and drawing strength from one's faith.

For leaders, whether guided by faith or personal values, the call to courage serves as a reminder of the higher responsibilities they bear and the impact their leadership can have on their communities. Courageous leadership is about aligning one's actions with deeper values and contributing to the greater good.

But faith-based courage is not just about personal strength—it's about prophetic action. It's about standing as a voice for the voiceless, challenging the powers that be, and leading the charge for justice and righteousness, even when the odds are stacked against you.

Conclusion

Leading with courage is essential for addressing the profound challenges facing South Africa and beyond. It involves a steadfast commitment to principles, resilience in the face of adversity, and empathy for others. But above all, it requires a radical commitment to truth and justice. By drawing inspiration from historical and contemporary examples of courageous leadership, embracing its core attributes, and fostering a supportive culture, we can navigate our challenges with integrity and drive meaningful change. Courageous leaders not only inspire action but also foster hope and possibility, paving the way for a more just and equitable society.

The question is not whether you can lead with courage—it's whether you will. Will you stand up in the face of adversity? Will you challenge the status quo? Will you take the risks necessary to drive the change that is so desperately needed? The future of our nation, our continent, and our world depends on those who dare to lead with courage.

Chapter 6: Embracing Diversity and Inclusion

The Essence of Embracing Diversity

Diversity and inclusion are not merely aspirational goals; they are the bedrock upon which a just and equitable society must be built. To embrace diversity means to recognize and value the myriad differences that each individual brings to the table—whether these differences are rooted in race, ethnicity, gender, socio-economic background, or other dimensions of identity. Inclusion is the mechanism through which these differences are not just acknowledged but celebrated, ensuring that every person feels respected, valued, and empowered to contribute.

Embracing diversity goes beyond token gestures and superficial representation. It requires a radical rethinking of how we interact with one another, how we build our institutions, and how we design our policies. It demands that we dismantle the structures that perpetuate inequality and create spaces where all voices are not only heard but amplified. This is not about charity or benevolence; it is about justice, equity, and the recognition that our strength as a society lies in our diversity.

In my various engagements across civic movements, academic institutions, and community organizations, I've seen firsthand the profound impact of truly embracing these principles. It is not about ticking boxes or meeting quotas; it is about weaving a rich tapestry of diverse voices into the very heart of our collective endeavors. This approach is not just a moral imperative—it is a strategic necessity for building a society that is resilient, innovative, and capable of addressing the complex challenges of our time.

Personal Insights and Lessons Learned

Reflecting on my experiences with the KZN Transformers and Pioneers, the commitment to embracing diversity was not a mere checkbox but a guiding principle that underpinned everything we did. Our mission to transform society through "Build, Grow, and Conquer" was deeply rooted in engaging with a wide spectrum of perspectives. This approach was crucial in moving beyond traditional methods to develop strategies that were more responsive and impactful.

A particularly telling example of this approach was our outreach in communities deeply affected by historical trauma. Initially, our strategies did not fully address the complexities faced by these communities. It was only through genuine engagement and listening to diverse perspectives that we were able to refine our approach and make a more meaningful impact. This experience underscored the importance of humility and the willingness to learn from those who are often marginalized or overlooked.

But embracing diversity is not without its challenges. It requires confronting uncomfortable truths about our own biases, prejudices, and blind spots. It demands that we step outside of our comfort zones and engage with perspectives that may challenge our assumptions and beliefs. This process can be difficult, but it is essential for personal growth and the development of a more inclusive and just society.

Ideological Differences: Challenges and Opportunities

Navigating ideological differences can be challenging, but it also offers invaluable opportunities for growth, innovation, and a richer understanding of our shared human experience. When we approach these differences with an open mind and a commitment to dialogue, we can transform potential conflicts into opportunities for deeper understanding and collaboration.

The work of Lindbong Development Group serves as a powerful model for addressing these challenges. Their efforts in promoting social cohesion, political tolerance, and coexistence demonstrate how ideological differences can be bridged through dialogue and collaboration. Their initiatives aim to create spaces where diverse voices are not only heard but actively engaged with, fostering environments where mutual respect and understanding can flourish.

For instance, Lindbong's approach to fostering dialogue between different community groups highlights the importance of addressing ideological differences head-on. By creating platforms for open and respectful conversations, they help bridge gaps and build a more cohesive society. This approach aligns with my belief in the power of dialogue as a tool for transformation. By facilitating open conversations about differences, we create opportunities for learning and growth, turning potential conflicts into avenues for deeper understanding and collaboration.

But let's not romanticize this process. Bridging ideological divides is hard work. It requires patience, empathy, and a willingness to confront difficult and sometimes painful truths. It demands that we move beyond the surface and engage with the underlying issues that drive division and conflict. This is not about seeking superficial consensus but about fostering genuine understanding and collaboration in the pursuit of common goals.

Confronting Systemic Challenges

Embracing diversity and inclusion also means confronting the deep-seated systemic issues that continue to plague our society. The legacy of apartheid in South Africa has left enduring scars that manifest in various forms: socio-economic disparities, fragmented communities, and a pervasive lack of national identity and patriotism. These challenges are not abstract; they are visible in the everyday lives of millions of South Africans. The absence of fathers, broken family units, and reckless lifestyles are symptoms of historical trauma that continue to reverberate through our society.

One of the most pernicious legacies of apartheid is the inter-tribal division that was intentionally fostered through the policy of Bantustanism. This policy, which segregated Black South Africans into homelands based on ethnicity, was designed to divide and weaken the population. The artificial tribal boundaries created by Bantustanism have left a legacy of mistrust, prejudice, and division that continues to affect our society today. These divisions are further exacerbated by the challenges of interprovincial migration, which has brought people from different tribal backgrounds into close proximity, often leading to tension and conflict. The legacy of Bantustanism and the realities of interprovincial migration have contributed to a fragmented society where unity is elusive and social cohesion is fragile.

Addressing these issues requires more than immediate interventions; it requires a comprehensive and radical approach that tackles the root causes of exclusion and inequality. This means confronting the systemic injustices that perpetuate poverty, marginalization, and social fragmentation. It means challenging the entrenched power structures that benefit from maintaining the status quo. It means acknowledging the historical and ongoing injustices that have shaped our society and taking bold action to redress them.

My work with different organizations has shown me that these systemic issues are formidable obstacles to achieving genuine inclusivity. The lack of trust between communities and authorities, ongoing social and economic disparities, and the persistence of historical grievances all pose significant challenges. Overcoming these obstacles necessitates a deep commitment to addressing historical injustices and fostering healing.

But let's be clear—this is not about making incremental changes or implementing superficial reforms. It is about dismantling the systems of oppression that continue to marginalize and exclude. It is about building a society where every person, regardless of their background or identity, has the opportunity to thrive.

Building an Inclusive Culture

Creating a truly inclusive culture involves more than policies and procedures; it requires a fundamental shift in mindset and practice. Leaders must champion diversity and inclusion, embedding these values into every aspect of their organizations. This means going beyond the rhetoric of inclusivity and taking concrete actions to create environments where diversity is not just accepted but celebrated.

Education and training on diversity are critical components of this process. Leaders and team members must be equipped with the skills to recognize and challenge biases, understand different cultural perspectives, and foster inclusivity. These training sessions are essential for shifting perspectives and creating an environment where diversity is not just accepted but celebrated.

Promoting open dialogue about diversity and inclusion is also crucial. Encouraging conversations on these topics helps build understanding and empathy, creating a safe space for individuals to express their concerns and share their experiences. This dialogue is key to building trust and fostering an inclusive culture.

But building an inclusive culture is not just the responsibility of leaders—it is the responsibility of everyone within the organization. Each of us must take ownership of our own biases and commit to creating a more inclusive and equitable environment. This means speaking out against discrimination and exclusion, challenging unfair practices, and actively working to build a culture of respect and inclusion.

The Role of Leadership in Driving Inclusion

Leaders play a vital role in advancing diversity and inclusion. Their actions and decisions set the tone for their organizations and influence their cultures. By demonstrating a commitment to these principles, leaders can inspire others to follow suit and work towards creating a more equitable environment.

Effective leaders must proactively address issues of exclusion and bias. They need to take responsibility for creating a culture that values diversity and inclusion, addressing issues as they arise and anticipating potential challenges.

Leaders should model the behaviors they wish to see, actively engaging with diverse communities and promoting inclusivity.

But let's push this further—leaders must be willing to take risks, to make bold decisions that challenge the status quo. They must be willing to confront the uncomfortable truths that often lie at the heart of exclusion and discrimination. They must be willing to use their power and influence to create real, lasting change.

Biblical Principles and Inclusive Vision

The importance of embracing diversity and inclusion is also reflected in biblical teachings. Ephesians 2:13-16 speaks to the heart of reconciliation and unity, stating:

"But now in Christ Jesus you who once were far away have been brought near by the blood of Christ. For he himself is our peace, who has made the two groups one and has destroyed the barrier, the dividing wall of hostility, by setting aside in his flesh the law with its commands and regulations. His purpose was to create in himself one new humanity out of the two, thus making peace, and in one body to reconcile both to God through the cross, by which he put to death their hostility."

This passage highlights the transformative power of inclusion and unity, reinforcing the idea that embracing diversity is central to building a more just and equitable society.

But let's not miss the radical nature of this message—Christ's vision was not one of superficial harmony but of deep, transformative reconciliation. It was about breaking down the walls that divide us, about creating a new humanity where all are equal and where peace is built on the foundation of justice and inclusion.

Stories of Transformation

In South Africa, various sectors have witnessed powerful examples of embracing diversity and inclusion. In politics, figures like Nelson Mandela and Desmond Tutu championed reconciliation and unity, transcending racial and ideological divides to build a democratic nation. Their leadership demonstrated how embracing diversity and fostering inclusivity can drive national transformation.

In the church, leaders like Nicholas Bengu, Dr. Michael Cassidy, Dr. Frank Chikane, and other apostolic figures have worked tirelessly to bridge denominational and cultural divides, promoting a vision of unity that reflects the inclusive nature of the gospel. Their efforts in fostering cross-cultural understanding and collaboration are a testament to the power of embracing diversity within religious contexts.

In the marketplace, African entrepreneurs and leaders are breaking new ground by creating inclusive business practices that value diverse perspectives and promote equitable opportunities. These leaders are shaping industries and economies while championing the principles of diversity and inclusion.

In recreational spaces, community initiatives and programs aim to bring people from different backgrounds together through shared activities and experiences. These efforts highlight the role of inclusion in fostering social cohesion and building stronger communities.

But these stories of transformation are not just about individual leaders—they are about movements, about collective efforts to create a society that is more just, more inclusive, and more equitable. They remind us that real change is possible when we embrace diversity, when we challenge exclusion, and when we work together to build a better future.

A Call to Action

Embracing diversity and inclusion is a continuous and evolving journey. It demands that we not only celebrate our differences but also actively address the systemic issues that perpetuate exclusion and inequality. As leaders, we must champion these values and drive meaningful change within our organizations and communities.

We must move beyond superficial engagement and work towards creating environments where diversity is not just acknowledged but actively promoted. This involves confronting historical injustices, building inclusive cultures, and fostering open dialogue. By doing so, we can create communities that are resilient, innovative, and compassionate.

In the upcoming chapter, we will explore the critical steps to building thriving and cohesive communities. This involves not just embracing diversity but also implementing strategies that foster social cohesion and collective growth. The journey towards inclusivity is intertwined with the broader goal of creating communities that thrive on collaboration and mutual respect. Join me as we delve into how we can turn our collective aspirations into tangible actions that build stronger, more connected communities.

Chapter 7: Building Thriving and Cohesive Communities

Vision for a Thriving Future

Building thriving and cohesive communities is not just a noble pursuit; it is a radical and revolutionary act of resistance against the forces that seek to divide, oppress, and marginalize. It is about challenging the systemic inequalities that have been engineered to keep communities fragmented and disempowered. This vision demands that we go beyond mere survival or temporary solutions—it requires us to create a legacy of sustainable growth and well-being that resonates for generations.

This journey is about more than just laying bricks or drafting policies; it is about dismantling the very structures that perpetuate injustice. It is about creating spaces where every individual, regardless of their background or circumstance, has the opportunity to not only survive but to thrive. It's about crafting a future where the bonds of community are stronger than the forces that seek to tear us apart.

The Essence of Community Cohesion

Community cohesion is not a passive state of being; it is an active, dynamic force that requires continuous cultivation. It is built on the radical notion that our differences, rather than dividing us, are the very source of our strength. In a truly cohesive community, people from all walks of life come together, not just to coexist but to collaborate in the pursuit of shared goals and a common purpose.

In South Africa, where the scars of apartheid, Bantustanism, and colonialism still run deep, the need for radical community cohesion is urgent. The legacy of inter-tribal division, exacerbated by the policy of Bantustanism, has left us with deep-seated mistrust and fragmented communities. This, combined with the challenges of interprovincial migration, has created a volatile mix that threatens the very fabric of our society.

But we must confront these challenges head-on. We must recognize that true community cohesion cannot be achieved through superficial means. It requires a radical reimagining of our social, political, and economic structures—a transformation that is rooted in justice, equity, and the unshakeable belief that we are stronger together than we could ever be apart.

Principles of Thriving Communities

1. **Radical Inclusivity and Participation:** Inclusivity must be more than a buzzword; it must be the foundation upon which our communities are built. Every voice, especially those that have been historically marginalized, must not only be heard but amplified. We must actively dismantle the barriers that prevent full participation and create spaces where everyone can contribute to the collective good. This is about more than just inviting people to the table—it's about building a new table that belongs to everyone.
2. **Shared Vision and Revolutionary Goals:** A thriving community is one that is united by a shared vision of justice, equity, and collective well-being. This vision must be radical in its scope, challenging the status quo and setting bold, revolutionary goals that reflect the aspirations of the entire community. This vision must be more than words on paper—it must be a living, breathing force that drives every action, decision, and policy.
3. **Empowerment and Capacity Building as Acts of Liberation:** Empowerment is not just about giving people tools and resources; it is about liberating them from the structures that have kept them oppressed. Capacity building should be viewed as a form of resistance—an act of defiance against the forces that seek to keep communities powerless. This means equipping individuals and groups with the skills, knowledge, and support they need to take control of their destinies and to lead their communities toward collective liberation.
4. **Collaborative and Courageous Leadership:** Leadership in a thriving community must be collaborative, courageous, and rooted in the principles of social justice. Leaders must be willing to confront uncomfortable truths, challenge entrenched power dynamics, and make decisions that prioritize the common good over personal gain. Collaborative leadership is not about compromise—it is about working together to achieve a vision of radical transformation.
5. **Resilience and Adaptability as Revolutionary Tools:** In a world that is constantly changing, communities must be resilient and adaptable. But resilience is not just about bouncing back from adversity—it is about transforming challenges into opportunities for growth and innovation. This requires a culture of continuous learning, critical reflection, and a willingness to adapt and evolve in the face of new realities.

Values and Experiences in Building Communities

My journey as a social engagement facilitator, development practitioner, and leadership coach has been shaped by the understanding that building thriving communities is an inherently radical act. It requires more than just good intentions—it demands a deep commitment to the principles of social justice, equity, and liberation.

- **Empathy and Radical Understanding:** True empathy goes beyond simply understanding another person's experiences—it requires a radical commitment to seeing the world through their eyes and standing with them in their struggles. As a social engagement facilitator, I've learned that empathy is the bedrock of solidarity, and solidarity is the foundation of community cohesion.
- **Strategic Development as Revolutionary Planning:** Strategic development must be rooted in a revolutionary vision of what is possible. It requires more than just planning; it requires the courage to dream big and the determination to turn those dreams into reality. As a development practitioner, I've seen firsthand how strategic planning can be a powerful tool for community empowerment when it is guided by a vision of radical transformation.
- **Leadership and Coaching as Acts of Empowerment:** Leadership is not about power—it is about empowering others to become leaders in their own right. Through coaching and training, I've worked to cultivate a new generation of leaders who are committed to the principles of social justice and who understand that true leadership is about serving the community.
- **Community-Centered Interventions as Catalysts for Change:** Community-centered interventions are not just about addressing immediate needs—they are about creating the conditions for long-term, sustainable change. These interventions must be driven by the community, for the community, and must be grounded in the principles of equity, justice, and inclusion.

Examples of Community-Driven Interventions

Across South Africa and beyond, there are countless examples of how community-driven interventions have transformed lives and created thriving, cohesive communities. These projects are proof that when communities come together, armed with a shared vision and the tools to achieve it, nothing is impossible.

From cooperative farming initiatives that tackle food insecurity to community centers that provide education and vocational training, these interventions have empowered individuals, strengthened community ties, and created pathways to a better future.

But these examples are just the beginning. The true potential of community-driven change is limitless when we commit to radical inclusivity, shared leadership, and a vision of collective liberation.

Processes for Building Thriving Communities

To build thriving and cohesive communities effectively, we must engage in processes that are as radical as our vision. These processes must be strategic, inclusive, and grounded in the principles of social justice and equity.

1. **Community Assessment as a Revolutionary Act:** Understanding the unique needs, strengths, and challenges of a community is the first step in any revolutionary journey. This requires more than just data collection—it demands deep engagement with community members, listening to their stories, and using those insights to inform strategies that are truly transformative.
2. **Strategic Planning for Radical Change:** Strategic planning must be more than just a roadmap—it must be a revolutionary manifesto. It should outline not only the goals and actions needed to achieve them but also the radical vision that drives the entire process. This plan must be bold, ambitious, and rooted in the principles of justice and equity.
3. **Engagement and Communication as Tools for Liberation:** Effective communication is the lifeblood of a cohesive community. It is through open, honest, and inclusive dialogue that we build trust, foster collaboration, and create a shared sense of purpose. Communication must be more than just an exchange of information—it must be a tool for empowerment and liberation.
4. **Implementation and Evaluation for Accountability:** Implementing strategies and monitoring progress is crucial for success, but this process must be rooted in accountability. We must be willing to critically evaluate our actions, learn from our mistakes, and make the necessary adjustments to stay true to our vision of radical transformation.
5. **Sustainability and Scaling as Acts of Resistance:** Focusing on sustainability ensures that our efforts have a lasting impact, but it also serves as a form of resistance against the forces that seek to undermine our progress. By planning for ongoing support and fostering community ownership, we can scale successful interventions and create a ripple effect of change that extends far beyond our immediate communities.

Biblical Principles and Community Building

The principles of social cohesion and community building are deeply reflected in biblical teachings. Proverbs 11:14 reminds us, "For lack of guidance a nation falls, but victory is won through many advisers." This verse speaks to the power of collective wisdom, collaboration, and shared leadership in achieving success.

But let us also remember that the teachings of Christ call us to a radical love that transcends all barriers. In Christ's vision, there is no room for exclusion or division—only for unity, justice, and peace. This is the foundation upon which we must build our communities—a foundation that is unshakeable, rooted in love, and driven by a commitment to justice for all.

Conclusion

Building thriving and cohesive communities is a radical, revolutionary act that requires a deep commitment to the principles of social cohesion, justice, and equity. It demands that we confront the systemic forces that seek to divide us and that we work tirelessly to create a society where everyone has the opportunity to thrive.

This is not just about building communities—it is about transforming them. It is about creating a world where justice and equity are not just ideals but lived realities. The time for incremental change is over. The time for radical, transformative action is now.

We must move forward with a shared vision, a commitment to radical inclusivity, and the courage to challenge the status quo. Together, we can build communities that are not only thriving and cohesive but that serve as beacons of hope and possibility for the entire world.

Chapter 8: Promoting and Championing Racial Reconciliation

Racial Reconciliation: A Cry from the Depths of Our Wounded Nation

Racial reconciliation in South Africa is not just a moral imperative—it is the urgent cry of a wounded nation still grappling with the deep, festering wounds of apartheid and colonialism. It is a call to confront the brutal truths of our history, not with the intention of moving on, but with the resolve to move forward—toward genuine healing, justice, and unity. This is not a polite dialogue; it is a radical confrontation with the past and a bold commitment to building a future where all South Africans can live in true equality and solidarity.

The Legacy of the TRC: Truth Without Justice?

The Truth and Reconciliation Commission (TRC) was a monumental step in South Africa's journey towards reconciliation. It was a pioneering effort to confront the atrocities of the past, allowing victims and perpetrators alike to tell their stories in the hope of national healing. However, as the years have passed, it has become increasingly clear that while the TRC succeeded in truth-telling, it fell short of delivering on its mandate of true reconciliation and justice.

For many who participated in the TRC, the process felt more like putting a plaster on a deep, infected wound rather than addressing the core of the rot. The commission focused heavily on uncovering the truth of what happened during the apartheid years, but it often lacked the mechanisms or the will to hold perpetrators accountable or to provide meaningful reparations to victims. The focus on amnesty for those who confessed their crimes, while perhaps necessary for political stability, left many feeling that justice had been sacrificed for the sake of reconciliation.

This failure has had profound repercussions. The lack of justice and accountability has meant that many of the systemic inequalities and social divisions entrenched during apartheid have persisted, if not worsened, in the years since the TRC. Economic disparities remain stark, spatial segregation is still a reality, and racial tensions continue to simmer just below the surface. For many black South Africans, the TRC did not bring the closure or the healing they desperately needed. Instead, it often felt like the commission simply reopened old wounds without providing the necessary tools for true healing.

The Radical Path to True Reconciliation

True reconciliation demands more than just truth-telling; it requires justice, accountability, and profound systemic change. It requires us to go beyond the surface level, beyond the polite conversations, and to dig deep into the roots of our divisions—economic, social, and psychological. It means confronting the uncomfortable realities of our present, as much as our past, and being willing to dismantle the structures that continue to perpetuate inequality and division.

At Lindbong Development, we are committed to this radical journey. Our mission is to challenge the status quo, to dismantle the systems of oppression that remain deeply embedded in our society, and to build a new South Africa—one where reconciliation is not just an aspiration but a lived reality for every citizen.

Economic and Spatial Disparities: The Unfinished Business of Reconciliation

One of the most glaring failures of the TRC was its inability to address the economic and spatial disparities that are the legacy of apartheid. These disparities are not just historical artifacts; they are the living, breathing reality for millions of South Africans who continue to be marginalized in their own country. The TRC, in its focus on individual acts of violence and abuse, largely ignored the broader, systemic violence of apartheid—the economic exploitation, the forced removals, the deliberate underdevelopment of black communities.

Today, these economic and spatial inequalities are as entrenched as ever. Wealth remains concentrated in the hands of a few, predominantly white, South Africans, while the majority of black South Africans continue to live in poverty. The spatial planning of apartheid, which segregated people based on race, continues to shape our cities and towns, with predominantly black communities often lacking basic services and infrastructure.

True reconciliation cannot happen while these disparities persist. We must address the root causes of these inequalities, not just their symptoms. This means rethinking our economic policies, our urban planning, and our social services. It means ensuring that all South Africans, regardless of their race or background, have access to the opportunities and resources they need to thrive.

Skills Transfer and Cross-Cultural Mentoring: Building Bridges to Reconciliation

Skills transfer and cross-cultural mentoring are essential tools in the fight for racial reconciliation. These initiatives are about more than just economic empowerment; they are about breaking down the barriers that divide us, creating opportunities for genuine connection and understanding across racial and cultural lines.

However, these programs must be designed with a deep understanding of the systemic barriers that have kept marginalized communities at the periphery for so long. This means going beyond superficial gestures and creating spaces where real, transformative relationships can develop. It means challenging the norms and expectations that have kept black South Africans, especially those from lower socio-economic backgrounds, out of the centers of power and influence.

Cross-cultural mentoring, in particular, has the potential to be a powerful force for reconciliation. By pairing individuals from different backgrounds, we can foster mutual understanding and respect, breaking down the stereotypes and prejudices that continue to divide us. But for these initiatives to be effective, they must be sustained and supported over the long term. They cannot be one-off projects; they must be part of a broader, ongoing effort to build a more inclusive and equitable society.

Continuous Tensions Between AmaZulu and Indians in KZN

The historical and ongoing tension between AmaZulu and Indians in KwaZulu-Natal represents a significant obstacle to racial reconciliation. This tension, often manifesting as a "cold war," is deeply rooted in the legacy of colonialism, apartheid, and economic competition. The relationship between these communities is marked by distrust, resentment, and periodic flare-ups of violence, particularly during times of crisis.

These tensions are often exacerbated by economic disparities and competition for resources. The Indian community in KZN, having been historically positioned in an intermediary role between white and black South Africans, often finds itself caught between the two. Economic success among Indians has sometimes been perceived by AmaZulu as having come at the expense of black South Africans, fueling animosity.

During times of political or economic crisis, these underlying tensions can explode into open conflict, as seen in the violent confrontations during the 1949 riots and, more recently, in the aftermath of the July 2021 unrest. These events reveal the fragility of the social fabric in KZN and the urgent need for reconciliation that addresses not just economic inequalities but also the deep-seated historical grievances and mistrust between these communities.

The Role of African Foreign Nationals in the Battle for Resources

The presence of African foreign nationals—whether economic migrants, illegal immigrants, asylum seekers, or refugees—has added another layer of complexity to South Africa's racial dynamics. These individuals, often fleeing dire circumstances in their home countries, come to South Africa seeking better opportunities. However, their arrival has sometimes sparked resentment and conflict, particularly in economically disadvantaged communities where competition for jobs, housing, and services is intense.

This tension is not just about resources; it is also about identity and belonging. African foreign nationals are often scapegoated for economic difficulties and are accused of taking jobs and opportunities from South Africans. This has led to xenophobic violence, which further strains the relationships between different racial and ethnic groups in the country.

The challenge of integrating African foreign nationals into South African society is significant. It requires not only legal and policy interventions but also efforts to foster understanding and solidarity between South Africans and their African brothers and sisters. Reconciliation in this context means recognizing the shared struggles of black people across the continent and working together to overcome the legacy of colonialism and apartheid that continues to divide us.

Internal Tensions Among Blacks, Whites, Indians, and Coloureds

The internal tensions among South Africa's racial groups—blacks, whites, Indians, and coloureds—are another major barrier to reconciliation. These tensions are often the result of historical grievances, economic competition, and the persistence of racial stereotypes and prejudices.

Among black South Africans, there is often a deep-seated frustration with the slow pace of economic transformation and the continued dominance of white South Africans in many areas of life. This frustration is sometimes directed not only at whites but also at Indians and coloureds, who are perceived as having been co-opted into the white power structure during apartheid.

For whites, there is often a fear of losing their privileged position in society, which can manifest as resistance to change and reluctance to fully engage in the reconciliation process. Meanwhile, the coloured community, which has historically been marginalized and caught between the black and white populations, often feels overlooked in discussions of racial justice and reconciliation.

These internal tensions are compounded by a lack of trust and understanding between the different racial groups. True reconciliation will require addressing these divisions head-on, fostering dialogue, and creating opportunities for people from different backgrounds to work together toward common goals.

Biblical Perspectives on Reconciliation: A Call to Justice and Peace

The Bible offers a profound framework for understanding reconciliation—not as a passive process, but as an active, radical pursuit of justice and peace. Ephesians 2:13-16 speaks to the heart of this journey: "But now in Christ Jesus you who once were far away have been brought near by the blood of Christ. For he himself is our peace, who has made the two groups one and has destroyed the barrier, the dividing wall of hostility... His purpose was to create in himself one new humanity out of the two, thus making peace."

This passage is not just about spiritual reconciliation; it is about social reconciliation, about the breaking down of the walls that divide us and the creation of a new, unified humanity. In South Africa, this biblical vision challenges us to go beyond surface-level reconciliation and to embrace a radical, transformative approach. It calls us to confront the systemic inequalities that continue to divide us and to work tirelessly to create a society where all people are valued, respected, and empowered.

One New Humanity: Faith in Action

One New Humanity, a church-driven initiative on building a church of racial and cultural diversity exemplifies how faith communities can lead the charge for racial and cultural reconciliation. This group of churches is committed to advancing God's Kingdom on earth through reconciliation, driven by the belief that being reconciled to God empowers believers, through the Holy Spirit, to reconcile with each other. This initiative transcends racial and cultural divides, creating platforms where believers can come together, not just in worship, but in action—addressing the deep-seated inequities that divide our society.

One New Humanity challenges us to live out our faith in practical ways, to go beyond the walls of the church, and to engage in the radical work of reconciliation. This is not just about talking; it is about doing—taking concrete steps to heal the wounds of the past and build a future where all people can live together in peace and justice.

Durban City Story: Connecting for Change

City Story represents a bold initiative aimed at transforming Durban into one of the most desired African cities to live in. This movement connects government, church, business, and citizens in a collective effort to effect change. It is a powerful example of how diverse sectors of society can come together to address the challenges of racial and economic inequality, working collaboratively to build a city that is inclusive, equitable, and vibrant.

City Story's mission aligns perfectly with the broader goals of racial reconciliation. By bringing together different stakeholders, it creates opportunities for dialogue, collaboration, and action—fostering an environment where reconciliation is not just an idea, but a lived reality. This initiative reminds us that reconciliation is not just about healing past wounds, but about building a future where everyone has a stake in the prosperity and well-being of their community.

Reconciliation is not a theoretical concept but a practical, on-the-ground reality that requires radical action. Recent initiatives in South Africa and beyond provide powerful examples of what can be achieved when we commit to this path.

The Responsibility of White and Indian South Africans in Reconciliation

Reconciliation is not just the responsibility of the marginalized; it requires active engagement from those who hold power and privilege. White and Indian South Africans must acknowledge their historical and current privileges and actively work toward dismantling systemic racism and building equitable systems. This goes beyond charity—it requires a deep commitment to structural changes that promote justice and equity.

These communities must recognize that true reconciliation involves a willingness to listen, learn, and engage in difficult conversations about privilege, power, and responsibility. It means moving beyond token gestures to become true allies in the fight for justice, supporting policies and initiatives that address systemic inequalities and empower marginalized communities.

The Role of Black and Coloured South Africans in Reconciliation

While black and coloured South Africans have borne the brunt of apartheid's injustices, they too have a critical role to play in reconciliation. This involves engaging in reconciliation not only with other racial groups but also within their communities, addressing internal divisions and fostering solidarity. It means working together to build a more just and equitable society, recognizing that true empowerment comes from collective action.

For black South Africans, this may involve challenging the internalized narratives of inferiority and self-destruction that apartheid sought to instill. It means rejecting the pursuit of whiteness and embracing a proud, empowered identity that values black culture, heritage, and community. For coloured South Africans, it involves asserting their unique identity and role in the reconciliation process, ensuring that their voices are heard and their contributions recognized.

A Call for National Unity

The path to racial reconciliation in South Africa is long, difficult, and fraught with challenges. But it is also profoundly necessary. The failures of the TRC have left deep scars on our national psyche, and the work of reconciliation remains unfinished. My experiences and strategic engagements highlight the need for a radical, systemic approach to this critical issue. Through deep engagement, confronting systemic inequalities, and fostering collaborative solutions, we can work toward a society where reconciliation is not just an aspiration but a tangible reality.

Let us embrace the principles of empathy, justice, and shared responsibility. Let us commit to the hard work of reconciliation, knowing that the journey will be difficult but that the rewards—unity, peace, and justice—are worth every effort. Together, we can build a future where every individual can thrive in an environment of unity and respect. The journey toward reconciliation is long and arduous, but with a comprehensive and relentless approach, we can overcome the legacies of the past and create a more equitable and harmonious society.

Chapter 9: Empowering the Youth

Empowering the youth is not merely an investment in the future; it is an urgent and radical necessity for advancing reconciliation, justice, and societal transformation in South Africa. The youth stand not only as inheritors of a tumultuous past but as the architects of our collective future. This chapter explores how harnessing the boundless energy, creativity, and idealism of young people can bridge racial divides, confront systemic failures, address unique challenges, and outline bold strategies to empower them as catalysts for profound change.

The Transformative Role of Youth in Racial Reconciliation

South Africa's youth embody the potential to challenge entrenched divisions and sculpt a more unified society. They stand at the crossroads of historical injustices and the promise of a future steeped in inclusivity and equity. This generation carries forward the legacy of resistance against apartheid while infusing the struggle with fresh perspectives and innovative solutions.

However, this potential is often undermined by a pervasive culture of instant gratification, driven by social media and the pressure to project an artificial image of success. The narrative of a "sad generation with happy pictures" underscores a tragic disconnect between the reality of youth struggles and the facade they feel compelled to maintain. Social media has become both a battleground and a cage, trapping the youth in a relentless pursuit of validation through likes, shares, and followers. This obsession with surface-level approval not only distracts from the deeper issues that need to be addressed but also traps many young people in cycles of superficiality, anxiety, and restlessness.

The restlessness and agitation of the youth, which could be powerful tools for change, are often misdirected, leading them into actions that do not serve their long-term interests. Instead of being harnessed to drive societal transformation, this energy is frequently exploited by those who seek to maintain the status quo, keeping the youth on the wrong side of the story of our continuous transition and recovery as a nation. This misdirection often manifests in fleeting trends, consumerist indulgence, and a constant search for the next dopamine hit, all of which detract from meaningful engagement with the structural challenges facing the country.

To counter this, it is crucial that we empower the youth to capture the vision for their future and actively participate in building it. This involves equipping them with the tools and knowledge they need to navigate the challenges of modern society, while also encouraging them to look beyond immediate gratification. We must challenge the prevailing narrative that equates success with material wealth and superficial status, instead promoting a vision of success that is rooted in social impact, collective upliftment, and genuine personal fulfillment.

Biblical Examples of Vision and Generational Leadership

The biblical narrative provides profound insights into the dynamic interplay between different generations in pursuing a shared vision. The stories of King David and King Solomon serve as powerful metaphors for understanding this relationship.

- **King David's Preparation**: King David's preparations for building the temple in Jerusalem illustrate the significance of laying a robust foundation for future leaders. David meticulously gathered resources, organized labor, and crafted a vision for Solomon to fulfill. This preparatory work was not just a legacy but a deliberate strategy to ensure the successful realization of a long-term vision (1 Chronicles 22:5-16). David understood that his reign was only one chapter in a much larger story—one that would unfold through the efforts of the next generation. His willingness to invest in a future he would not see exemplifies the selflessness required of leaders who are truly committed to the long-term good of their people.
- **King Solomon's Leadership**: Despite his youth and inexperience, Solomon embraced the vision bestowed upon him by David. His leadership in constructing the temple symbolizes the energy and potential of the younger generation. Solomon's success in this monumental task underscores the importance of empowering young leaders to harness their skills, talents, and enthusiasm in achieving collective goals (1 Kings 6). Solomon's ability to build on David's foundation and take the vision to completion is a powerful reminder of the importance of continuity and generational collaboration in leadership.

These stories remind us of the importance of preparing the next generation to take over the mantle of leadership. Just as David laid the groundwork for Solomon, we must provide our youth with the resources, support, and vision they need to lead effectively. We must guide them in capturing the vision of a more inclusive and just society, empowering them to carry it forward with the same determination and purpose. The failure to prepare the next generation is not just a missed opportunity; it is a dereliction of duty that leaves our society vulnerable to stagnation and decline.

Challenges Facing South Africa's Youth

While the youth hold immense potential, they face formidable challenges that impede their full participation in societal transformation. Addressing these challenges is critical for unleashing their power to effect change.

- **Educational Inequities**: The disparities in access to quality education remain a significant barrier. Many young South Africans, particularly those from marginalized communities, are denied the educational opportunities necessary for personal and professional development. The lack of adequate infrastructure and resources exacerbates these inequities, leaving a substantial portion of the youth population at a disadvantage. This systemic failure continues to perpetuate cycles of poverty and limited access to opportunities, stifling the potential of countless young individuals. The education system, as it currently stands, often replicates the very inequalities it should be dismantling. The curriculum is often out of touch with the realities of the majority of South Africans, failing to equip young people with the skills they need to thrive in a rapidly changing world. Moreover, the emphasis on rote learning and standardized testing stifles creativity and critical thinking, which are essential for addressing the complex challenges we face.
- **Unemployment, Underemployment, and Economic Exclusion**: High youth unemployment rates, compounded by economic inequalities and limited job prospects, marginalize young people from meaningful economic participation. Underemployment further exacerbates this issue, as many young South Africans are forced into low-paying, unstable, or part-time jobs that do not utilize their skills or offer career advancement. The absence of stable employment opportunities prevents them from contributing fully to the economy and achieving financial independence, stifling their ability to drive economic innovation and entrepreneurial endeavors. The economic system remains skewed in favor of those who already have access to capital and networks, leaving the majority of young people on the outside looking in. This exclusion not only denies them the opportunity to build wealth but also reinforces feelings of alienation and disenfranchisement, fueling social unrest.
- **Instant Gratification and the Pressure of Social Media**: The modern youth are inundated with images of success and wealth on social media, leading to an unhealthy pursuit of instant gratification. This artificial lifestyle creates immense pressure to conform to unrealistic standards, which can distract from the real issues that need to be addressed. The pursuit of surface-level success often overshadows the deeper, more meaningful work of building a life and a society based on substance, values, and long-term vision. The commodification of identity

and the relentless push for consumerism have turned social media into a marketplace where self-worth is measured by material possessions and social status. This not only distorts the values of the youth but also perpetuates a cycle of consumption that is both unsustainable and spiritually bankrupt.
- **Social and Political Divisions**: Generational gaps and cultural differences often create tensions between the experienced older generation and the younger, more idealistic leaders. This divide can hinder the effectiveness of reconciliation efforts and delay the implementation of progressive changes. The friction between traditional and radical approaches to social and political issues underscores the need for dialogue and collaboration across generational lines. The older generation, having fought and sacrificed for freedom, often finds it difficult to understand the impatience and disillusionment of the youth, who are frustrated by the slow pace of change and the persistence of inequality. Meanwhile, the youth, in their zeal to disrupt and innovate, may overlook the hard-won lessons of the past. Bridging this divide requires mutual respect, a willingness to listen, and a shared commitment to the principles of justice and equality.
- **The Burden of Family Responsibility**: A particularly tragic reality for many black youth is the expectation that they must liberate their parents from poverty before they can begin to build their own lives. This expectation places an enormous burden on young people, who are often forced to delay their own dreams and aspirations to fulfill the financial and emotional needs of their families. This is exacerbated by a cultural narrative that glorifies the idea of children being the breadwinners, a notion that must be challenged and rejected. Parents should work to ensure that their children have a solid foundation to build from, rather than relying on them as a source of income and livelihood. This dynamic perpetuates a cycle of poverty and dependency that is difficult to break. Instead of being able to invest in their own futures, young people are forced to take on the role of providers at a time when they should be focusing on their education and personal development.

Proverbs 13:22 states, "A good man leaves an inheritance to his children's children." This scripture emphasizes the importance of parents working to provide for the next generation, ensuring that they have the resources and support they need to thrive. It is a call to parents to take responsibility for their own financial well-being and to build a legacy that their children can build upon, rather than placing the burden on their children to support them. Parents must be the ones to break the cycle of poverty and deprivation, setting the stage for their children to achieve even greater heights.

Strategies for Radical Youth Empowerment

To unlock the transformative potential of South Africa's youth, a multifaceted and radical approach is required. This approach must address their diverse needs and aspirations while challenging existing barriers to their success.

1. **Education and Skills Development**: Enhancing access to quality education and vocational training is fundamental. We must overhaul the education system to provide equitable opportunities for all young people. Investing in skills development programs will equip the youth with the competencies needed for personal growth and leadership. These initiatives should not only focus on academic knowledge but also on critical thinking, problem-solving, and innovative thinking. Education should be a tool for liberation, not just a means of producing workers for the economy. It should empower young people to think critically about the world around them, to question the status quo, and to imagine new possibilities for their communities and for the country.
2. **Entrepreneurship and Innovation**: Fostering an entrepreneurial culture among the youth is vital. Through mentorship programs, startup incubators, and accessible funding opportunities, we can empower young people to create sustainable businesses and drive economic innovation. Encouraging entrepreneurship helps combat unemployment and fosters a culture of self-reliance and creativity. However, this must go beyond mere rhetoric. The barriers to entrepreneurship—such as access to capital, market opportunities, and networks—must be systematically dismantled. We need to create an ecosystem that nurtures and supports young entrepreneurs, particularly those from marginalized communities, enabling them to build businesses that contribute to the common good.
3. **Civic Engagement and Leadership**: Promoting active participation in civic and political processes is essential for nurturing responsible citizenship. Leadership development initiatives and community service projects can cultivate a sense of advocacy for social justice and community engagement. By involving youth in decision-making processes, we ensure that their voices are heard and valued in shaping the future of the nation. Civic engagement should not be seen as an optional extra but as a core component of youth development. Young people must be equipped with the skills and knowledge to engage critically with political processes, to advocate for their rights, and to hold those in power accountable. This requires not just education but also opportunities for meaningful participation in decision-making at all levels of society.
4. **Digital Literacy and Technology**: Expanding access to digital literacy programs and technological resources is crucial for empowering the youth

in the digital age. Providing internet connectivity and technological tools enables them to leverage digital platforms for education, communication, and economic opportunities. This digital empowerment is key to bridging the digital divide and fostering innovation. However, digital literacy must go beyond basic skills. It must include critical thinking about the role of technology in society, the ethical implications of digital platforms, and the ways in which technology can be harnessed for social good. Young people must be empowered to use technology not just as consumers but as creators and innovators, capable of shaping the digital future in ways that align with their values and aspirations.

5. **Arts and Culture**: Investing in arts and cultural initiatives provides platforms for creative expression and cultural exchange. Celebrating diversity through arts helps foster dialogue and understanding across racial and cultural boundaries. Cultural initiatives also offer young people opportunities to engage in meaningful ways that bridge divides and promote unity. The arts should be seen not just as a form of entertainment but as a powerful tool for social change. Through music, literature, visual arts, and performance, young people can explore and express complex issues related to identity, culture, and social justice. Cultural initiatives can also play a crucial role in preserving and revitalizing indigenous languages and traditions, helping to build a sense of pride and belonging among young people.

These strategies are not mere recommendations but essential steps toward a radical reimagining of our societal structures. My own efforts in youth engagement and empowerment have demonstrated the profound impact of these approaches. By addressing educational and economic barriers and fostering a culture of innovation and civic participation, we can unleash the full potential of our young leaders.

Generational Leadership and Collaboration

Building bridges between generations is essential for sustainable societal transformation. This collaboration requires mutual respect and a shared vision for reconciliation and progress.

- **Respect for Experience**: It is crucial to acknowledge the wisdom and experience of older generations. Their historical knowledge and understanding of the complexities of reconciliation are invaluable. Respecting their contributions while seeking to integrate youthful energy and ideas creates a balanced and effective approach to societal change. The older generation has much to teach us about resilience, perseverance, and the long-term struggle for justice. Their experiences

can provide invaluable lessons for navigating the challenges of today. At the same time, the youth bring fresh perspectives, new ideas, and a willingness to challenge the status quo. By combining these strengths, we can develop strategies that are both innovative and grounded in the hard-won lessons of history.
- **Empowerment of Youth**: Empowering the youth involves creating opportunities for them to contribute their innovative ideas and passion for justice. By providing platforms for youth leadership and ensuring they have the resources and support needed, we harness their potential for transformative impact. This means not only listening to young people but also actively involving them in decision-making processes. It means creating spaces where their voices are heard and their contributions valued. It also means providing them with the tools and resources they need to succeed, whether that be through education, mentorship, or access to capital.
- **Collaborative Vision**: A shared vision of reconciliation and social cohesion must transcend generational divides. By leveraging the strengths and perspectives of both older and younger leaders, we can develop comprehensive strategies for addressing societal challenges and achieving collective goals. This requires a commitment to ongoing dialogue and collaboration, as well as a willingness to learn from one another. It also requires a shared commitment to the values of justice, equality, and human dignity, which must guide all of our efforts to build a better future.

In my work with various institutions and organizations, the collaboration between different generations has been a driving force for progress. By creating environments where youth and experienced leaders can work together, we not only address immediate challenges but also build a foundation for long-term transformation.

The Imperative of Realizing a Generational Mission

South Africa's future hinges on realizing the generational mission of integrating youthful energy with experienced wisdom. Empowering the youth to lead is not just a strategic move but a fundamental necessity for overcoming historical injustices and building a just society. This integration involves addressing educational inequities, fostering entrepreneurship, promoting civic engagement, and embracing cultural diversity.

Empowering South Africa's youth is essential for achieving a more inclusive and equitable society. By addressing educational inequities, fostering entrepreneurship, promoting civic engagement, and celebrating cultural diversity, we can unlock the potential of young people as catalysts for transformative change. Through collaborative efforts between generations, rooted in mutual respect and a shared vision, we can build a brighter future for all South Africans.

A Call to Parents and Guardians

This chapter would be incomplete without addressing the role of parents and guardians in this transformative journey. The sad reality for many black youth is the expectation that they must liberate their parents from poverty before they can begin to build their own lives. This burden is not only unfair but detrimental to the development of the youth and the future of our society. Parents must be the ones to build and work to ensure that the next generation has a solid foundation from which to grow. The burden of providing for the family should not fall on the shoulders of the young; instead, they should be empowered to pursue their dreams and aspirations without the weight of familial expectations holding them back.

As Proverbs 13:22 wisely states, "A good man leaves an inheritance to his children's children." This scripture calls on parents to take responsibility for their own financial well-being and to build a legacy that their children can build upon, rather than placing the burden on their children to support them. It is a call to parents to work tirelessly to ensure that their children do not have to start from scratch but can instead build on the foundation laid by previous generations.

Conclusion

The journey towards youth empowerment demands bold actions, radical thinking, and an unwavering commitment to justice and reconciliation. By investing in our youth, we pave the way for a unified, just, and equitable South Africa. We must challenge the culture of instant gratification, dismantle the barriers to opportunity, and build bridges between generations. The future of our nation depends on our ability to empower the youth to take the reins and lead us into a brighter, more just future.

By empowering the youth, challenging the pressures of instant gratification, and fostering a collaborative vision across generations, we can transform South Africa into a nation where every young person has the opportunity to succeed. The journey is long and fraught with challenges, but it is a journey we must undertake with urgency, courage, and a relentless commitment to the principles of justice, equality, and human dignity.

The time to act is now. Let us empower the youth to be the leaders they are destined to be, to build the future they deserve, and to create a society where everyone can thrive, regardless of their background or circumstances. The legacy we leave for future generations depends on the actions we take today. Let us ensure that it is a legacy of justice, reconciliation, and true empowerment.

Chapter 10: Faith-Inspired Leadership: Transforming Society with Unshakable Conviction

Faith-inspired leadership is not a passive or peripheral concept; it is a dynamic and transformative force that can reshape societies and challenge entrenched norms. In South Africa, a nation grappling with profound issues of justice, reconciliation, and inequality, faith must serve as the cornerstone for leaders who envision and implement radical change. This chapter explores how faith infuses leadership with purpose, power, and a relentless drive for societal impact, urging leaders to let their faith guide their actions, decisions, and interactions. The ultimate goal is to integrate faith into every facet of leadership, ensuring it drives transformation beyond the walls of faith communities and into the very fabric of society.

Faith as a Catalyst for Radical Transformation

Faith is not just a personal conviction—it is a radical, disruptive force that compels us to challenge the status quo and drive profound societal change. It is a fire that burns within, pushing us to confront systemic injustices, to tear down the walls of oppression, and to build a society that reflects the values of justice, equity, and compassion. Faith does not allow us to be complacent or silent in the face of wrong; it demands action, courage, and unwavering commitment.

In my experience as a Bible-believing leader and social engagement practitioner, faith has been the driving force behind my efforts to address systemic issues and empower marginalized communities. Faith is not about simply declaring one's beliefs—it is about allowing those beliefs to shape every aspect of our leadership, from our strategic decisions to our daily interactions. Faith inspires us to envision a society where justice reigns and where the marginalized are uplifted, and it drives us to work tirelessly towards that vision.

In South Africa, where societal challenges such as inequality, injustice, and division persist, faith-inspired leadership requires a radical shift in how we approach these issues. It demands that we transcend conventional boundaries and integrate faith-driven principles into every aspect of our leadership. This integration means that our faith informs not just our personal actions but our strategic decisions and interactions with others, guiding us to work towards a more just and equitable society.

The Role of Prophetic Leadership

Faith-inspired leadership must go beyond traditional roles—it must embrace the mantle of prophetic leadership. Prophetic leaders are those who, driven by their faith, speak truth to power, challenge injustices, and call for radical societal transformation. This form of leadership is not just about guiding a community but about confronting and dismantling oppressive systems, no matter the cost.

The biblical prophets, such as Amos and Micah, are profound examples of prophetic leadership. Amos condemned the social injustices of his time, calling out the exploitation of the poor and the corruption of the powerful. Micah famously declared, "What does the Lord require of you? To act justly and to love mercy and to walk humbly with your God" (Micah 6:8). These prophets were not just spiritual leaders; they were voices of radical change, challenging the status quo and advocating for a society aligned with divine justice.

In today's context, faith leaders must adopt this prophetic stance, using their platforms to advocate for systemic change, social justice, and moral integrity. This means confronting uncomfortable truths within our organizations, communities, and broader societal structures. Faith-inspired leaders must not shy away from challenging the powers that be, even when it comes at a personal cost.

Addressing the Failures of Faith Communities

It is essential to confront the uncomfortable truth that faith communities have not always been on the side of justice. There have been times when religious institutions were complicit in systems of oppression, such as apartheid in South Africa, providing theological justifications for the regime's policies. This complicity highlights the danger of faith communities aligning with oppressive systems rather than challenging them.

During apartheid, some Christian denominations justified racial segregation and perpetuated the myth of white supremacy. This tragic chapter in our history reminds us that faith communities can become instruments of oppression if they fail to critically examine their teachings and practices. But this history also calls us to action—it demands that we confront and rectify these legacies. Faith leaders today must ensure that their teachings and practices promote inclusivity, justice, and reconciliation, rather than division or complacency.

Faith communities must reject the temptation to become insular, focusing only on internal growth rather than engaging with and transforming society. They must be at the forefront of the struggle for justice, advocating for the marginalized, and holding the powerful accountable. Faith cannot be a private matter—it must be a public force for good, challenging the systems that perpetuate inequality and injustice.

The Challenge of Dualism in Faith Practice

A significant challenge in faith-inspired leadership is the issue of dualism—where individuals separate their spiritual lives from their everyday actions and decisions. This dualism leads to a disconnection between faith and leadership, where leaders may profess strong religious beliefs but fail to apply these principles in their professional and public lives.

The Epistle of James emphasizes that "faith without works is dead" (James 2:14-26). This passage challenges believers to live out their faith in tangible ways, integrating their beliefs into every aspect of their lives. Leaders are called to embody their faith not just in their private lives but in their public actions and decisions. There can be no separation between what we believe and how we lead. Our faith must be evident in our commitment to justice, equity, and compassion in every sphere of our influence.

The Role of Faith in Economic Justice

Faith-inspired leadership must also address the critical issue of economic justice. In a country like South Africa, where poverty, unemployment, and economic inequality are rampant, faith must compel leaders to advocate for fairness, generosity, and stewardship.

The Year of Jubilee, as outlined in Leviticus 25, provides a radical biblical model for economic justice. Every fifty years, debts were forgiven, slaves were freed, and land was returned to its original owners. This principle reflects a deep commitment to economic equity, ensuring that no one remains perpetually oppressed or disadvantaged.

Faith-inspired leaders must advocate for policies and practices that reflect the principles of the Jubilee. This involves supporting initiatives that promote fair wages, equitable distribution of resources, and opportunities for economic advancement for marginalized communities. It also means challenging economic systems that perpetuate inequality and working towards a society where everyone has the opportunity to thrive.

Encouraging Active Participation in Social Movements

Faith leaders and communities must actively participate in social justice movements. It is not enough to support these movements from the pulpit or in private prayer; it involves taking to the streets, engaging in advocacy, and using their influence to bring about tangible change.

Rev. Dr. Martin Luther King Jr. is a powerful example of faith in action. His leadership in the Civil Rights Movement was deeply rooted in his Christian faith. He not only preached about justice but also led marches, organized protests, and spoke out against racial and economic injustices. His faith was not confined to the church but was actively engaged in the struggle for civil rights.

Faith leaders in South Africa and beyond are encouraged to engage directly with social movements, using their platforms to mobilize communities, advocate for policy changes, and support those who are fighting for justice and equality. This can involve partnerships with secular organizations, participation in protests and campaigns, and using religious spaces as centers for organizing and activism.

Reimagining Faith-Inspired Leadership for the Future

Faith-inspired leadership must not be static—it must be dynamic, innovative, and forward-thinking. Leaders must be open to new forms of leadership that break away from traditional models, embracing innovation and being willing to take bold, unconventional steps to address contemporary challenges.

This might involve embracing new technologies, social media, and other modern tools to reach broader audiences and advocate for change. Faith leaders can use these platforms to engage with younger generations, address contemporary issues, and mobilize global support for justice initiatives.

Leaders must reimagine how they can adapt their leadership to meet the needs of the 21st century. This involves thinking creatively about how to integrate faith and activism in a rapidly changing world, forming global alliances, and exploring new ways to inspire and mobilize people for the cause of justice and equity.

Biblical and Historical Exemplars of Faith-Fueled Leadership

Faith-inspired leadership is deeply rooted in the examples of biblical and historical figures whose lives and actions were guided by their unwavering convictions:

- **Moses:** His leadership in liberating the Israelites from Egyptian bondage exemplifies faith-driven courage and resilience. Moses' unwavering belief in God's promises allowed him to confront Pharaoh and lead his people through the wilderness despite enormous obstacles. His story is a testament to how faith can inspire radical action and perseverance in the face of seemingly insurmountable challenges.
- **Nehemiah:** The rebuilding of Jerusalem's walls under Nehemiah's leadership was not just a physical reconstruction but a profound act of faith and communal revival. Nehemiah's strategic planning, coupled with his fervent prayers and rallying of the people, illustrates how faith can drive a collective effort towards a common goal. His ability to mobilize the community and overcome significant opposition underscores the transformative power of faith-driven leadership in achieving substantial and lasting impact.
- **Jesus Christ:** His model of servant leadership was revolutionary, challenging societal norms and advocating for the marginalized. Jesus' teachings and actions were rooted in a profound sense of divine purpose and love for humanity. By challenging oppressive systems and promoting justice and compassion, Jesus' leadership serves as a powerful example of how faith can drive radical change and inspire others to follow a path of righteousness and service.
- **Prof. John Volmink:** A respected academic and education leader, Prof. Volmink has consistently integrated his Christian faith into his work, advocating for educational equity and justice. His leadership in various educational initiatives reflects a deep commitment to creating opportunities for marginalized communities and addressing systemic inequities through faith-driven action.
- **Dr. Frank Chikane:** As a former director-general in the presidency of South Africa and a prominent church leader, Dr. Chikane has consistently emphasized the role of faith in promoting justice, reconciliation, and ethical governance. His work in both the church and government sectors highlights the importance of faith-driven leadership in addressing societal challenges and promoting national unity.

Principles of Faith-Inspired Leadership

Faith-inspired leadership must be grounded in principles that reflect the depth and power of faith:

- **Integrity and Moral Courage:** Faith-driven leadership is rooted in unwavering integrity and moral courage. It calls leaders to uphold ethical standards and act with honesty, transparency, and accountability. In my own work, whether negotiating conflicts or

facilitating community development, faith compels me to adhere to these principles, even when faced with significant challenges. This commitment not only fosters trust and respect but also challenges systemic corruption and promotes a culture of accountability and ethical conduct.
- **Compassion and Empathy:** Compassion is a radical principle that demands more than mere sympathy. It requires active efforts to uplift and empower the marginalized and vulnerable. Faith-driven leaders prioritize inclusive practices and advocate for policies that promote social justice and human dignity. My engagement with diverse communities is driven by a deep empathy that goes beyond surface-level interactions, aiming to address systemic inequalities and promote holistic social change.
- **Servant Leadership:** The model of servant leadership, exemplified by Jesus Christ, involves prioritizing the needs of others and selflessly serving them. This approach challenges traditional notions of leadership and emphasizes humility, empathy, and a commitment to the common good. In my leadership practice, I strive to embody these principles by empowering others and supporting initiatives that drive collective advancement. Servant leadership is about focusing on the growth and development of those we lead, ensuring that our actions contribute to their success and well-being.
- **Visionary and Transformative Leadership:** Faith inspires a vision of what is possible beyond current limitations. It drives leaders to articulate a compelling vision for a just and equitable society and to mobilize communities towards achieving that vision. My vision of building a great life for this generation and beyond is rooted in a faith-driven understanding that transformation is both achievable and essential. This vision fuels my efforts to challenge existing structures and create innovative solutions for societal issues.

Discernment and Understanding Times and Seasons

The Sons of Issachar, known for their understanding of the times and knowledge of what needed to be done (1 Chronicles 12:32), exemplify the radical necessity of discernment in leadership. Faith empowers leaders to discern God's will and navigate complex challenges with strategic clarity. This discernment involves understanding the nuances of each situation and making decisions that align with a divine purpose.

Discernment is not just about recognizing opportunities but also about understanding the broader context and implications of our actions. Faith provides the guidance needed to make informed decisions that reflect a higher purpose and contribute to meaningful change. It requires leaders to remain attuned to both the immediate and long-term impacts of their decisions.

The Sons of Zebulon, known for their action-oriented approach, complement the discernment of Issachar by translating vision into tangible results. This synergy between vision and action is crucial for effective leadership, ensuring that strategic insights are implemented with practical outcomes.

The Role of Faith in Balancing and Breaking Stereotypes

Faith provides a radical framework for balancing societal issues and breaking down stereotypes. It challenges us to see beyond superficial differences and recognize the divine purpose in every individual. This perspective fosters a deeper understanding of humanity's shared worth and potential, transcending conventional biases and promoting inclusivity.

Faith encourages leaders to confront and dismantle stereotypes by emphasizing our common humanity and divine purpose. It inspires actions that reflect a commitment to justice, equity, and compassion, challenging societal norms and fostering a culture of respect and understanding.

Faith as a Source of Trust and Hope

Faith instills a profound trust and hope in the possibility of change. It is not just about believing that things will improve but actively working towards that change with conviction and perseverance. My personal journey is a testament to this belief, where trust in God's guidance has shaped my vision for development and empowered me to pursue a greater purpose that extends beyond conventional boundaries.

Faith provides the anchor that sustains us through challenges and uncertainties. It offers clarity of vision and purpose, enabling leaders to navigate complex environments with confidence and hope. This trust in divine guidance ensures that our efforts are aligned with a higher purpose and contribute to meaningful transformation.

Integrating Faith into All Spheres of Leadership

Faith-inspired leadership involves integrating spiritual principles into every aspect of our roles:

- **Prayer and Reflection:** These practices are essential for seeking divine guidance and clarity. They ground our decisions in a spiritual context, ensuring that every action aligns with a higher purpose. Prayer and reflection help leaders remain attuned to their divine calling and navigate challenges with discernment and grace.
- **Ethical Conduct:** Faith-driven principles guide us to uphold ethical standards in all aspects of leadership. This commitment to integrity, transparency, and accountability ensures that our actions reflect our values and inspire trust among stakeholders. Ethical conduct is a cornerstone of faith-inspired leadership, promoting a culture of respect and responsibility.
- **Community Engagement:** Engaging with diverse stakeholders fosters unity and collaborative problem-solving. Faith-driven leaders work to address societal issues through collective efforts, promoting social cohesion and collective well-being. Community engagement ensures that our leadership efforts are inclusive and address the needs of all individuals.

Conclusion

Faith-inspired leadership is a radical call to embody divine principles in every sphere of influence. It challenges us to integrate our faith into our actions, decisions, and interactions, driving societal transformation with conviction and integrity. By embracing faith as a guiding force, leaders can inspire hope, foster unity, and champion justice and compassion. This chapter emphasizes that faith, when lived out boldly and authentically, becomes a transformative power that shapes a more just, equitable, and compassionate society. Through our leadership, we reflect the authority and kingdom of the Creator, advancing humanity and fulfilling our divine mandate.

Chapter 11: Political Leadership for the Common Good

South Africa's political leadership stands at a crossroads, where the demands for genuine transformation have never been more urgent. The promises of democracy and the pursuit of equity have largely gone unfulfilled, leaving a nation grappling with deep-seated corruption, misaligned priorities, and a widening gap between those in power and the people they claim to serve. This chapter demands a radical reckoning with the harsh realities of our political system. It advocates for a leadership that not only serves the common good but also rejects the complacency of the status quo and confronts the systemic issues that hinder true progress. The path forward requires a seismic shift—a movement away from partisan self-interest and toward a political culture committed to justice, equity, and genuine public service.

The Betrayal of Trust Between Political Parties and Communities

The erosion of trust between political parties and the citizens they represent is not merely a problem; it is a crisis that threatens the very foundation of our democracy. Elected officials routinely make grand promises during election campaigns, only to abandon them once they ascend to power. This betrayal is not just about failed commitments; it is about a systemic failure where political priorities are skewed toward preserving power rather than addressing the urgent needs of the populace. Communities are left to contend with underfunded services, crumbling infrastructure, and a pervasive sense of disillusionment.

Throughout my extensive engagements with various communities and sectors, I have witnessed firsthand the destructive impact of this betrayal. Resources and opportunities are often concentrated among party loyalists rather than distributed based on need or merit. This selective allocation creates division and perpetuates inequality, reinforcing the very disparities that democracy was supposed to eliminate. It is time for leaders to confront this betrayal directly, to realign their focus on genuine public service, and to ensure that every community reaps the benefits promised by our democratic ideals.

The Corruption of Capital and the Weakening of the People's Will

Capital's stranglehold on politics represents a corruption that infects every aspect of governance. Money influences decisions, skews policy priorities, and distorts the democratic process, resulting in a political environment where financial power often overrides public interest. This leads to policies that benefit the wealthy and well-connected while leaving the majority marginalized and disillusioned.

Throughout my career, I have observed how financial power increasingly dictates the election of leaders, sidelining the needs and aspirations of the people. Infighting within political organizations and the rise of questionable characters who prioritize personal gain over public service further exacerbate this issue. Leaders who enter politics with noble intentions are often co-opted by capital, compromising their values and undermining their commitment to their communities. The system's failure to address this issue not only erodes public trust but also stifles meaningful progress. It is imperative that we confront the corrupting influence of capital head-on, demanding transparency, accountability, and a return to policies that genuinely serve the public good.

The Manipulation of Electoral Promises and the Poor Quality of Civic Engagement

The manipulation of electoral promises is not a minor issue but a fundamental betrayal of the democratic process. Politicians frequently use compelling rhetoric to garner votes, only to renege on their promises once elected. This pattern of deception damages public trust and fosters a cynical view of politics as a game of empty promises and ulterior motives.

The gap between political promises and actual delivery is a significant source of frustration and disillusionment among citizens. The disconnect between what is promised and what is delivered creates a cycle of disengagement, where citizens feel powerless and disconnected from the political process. To break this cycle, we must foster a culture of accountability, where leaders are held responsible for their promises and citizens are actively engaged in holding them accountable. This shift requires a concerted effort to educate the public about their role in the political process and to rebuild trust through transparent and honest governance.

Addressing Systemic Racism in Political Leadership

The political landscape in South Africa remains deeply scarred by the legacy of apartheid. Systemic racism continues to influence who holds power and how decisions are made, perpetuating inequality and division. Political leaders often fail to challenge these structures, instead of perpetuating them through their actions or inactions.

To address these entrenched issues, we must call for a new generation of leaders who are not only anti-racist in rhetoric but also in action. This involves dismantling racial hierarchies within government and public institutions and implementing policies that explicitly aim to promote equity and justice for all South Africans. The time has come for leaders to confront the realities of systemic racism and to take bold, decisive action to eradicate it from our political system.

Highlighting the Failure of Transformation Policies

South Africa has implemented various policies aimed at transformation, such as Black Economic Empowerment (BEE), but these policies have often failed to achieve true equity. Instead, they have sometimes been co-opted by elites, both black and white, who use them to entrench their own power rather than to uplift the broader population.

A complete overhaul of these policies is necessary. They must be restructured to genuinely benefit the marginalized and disenfranchised, rather than entrenching a new elite class. Transparency and accountability in the implementation of these policies are critical. We must demand that transformation initiatives are designed and executed in a way that truly addresses the systemic inequalities that continue to plague our society.

The Role of Civil Society and Grassroots Movements

Civil society and grassroots movements have always played a crucial role in holding political leaders accountable. These movements are often the first to identify and challenge injustices, pushing for change when the government fails to act.

It is time for a more active, even radical, engagement from civil society. Change will not come from within the political system alone; it requires sustained pressure from outside it. Civil disobedience, direct action, and grassroots organizing are all essential tools in the fight for accountability and justice. Civil society must be prepared to take bold, uncompromising action to demand the changes that our political leaders are unwilling to make.

Youth Leadership and Intergenerational Dynamics

South Africa's political system often sidelines younger voices, despite their potential to drive innovation and change. The lack of generational diversity in politics stifles progress and perpetuates outdated ideas and practices.

We must demand that political parties and institutions make space for younger leaders. The older generation of leaders who cling to power and resist change must be held accountable for their failures. A generational shift in leadership is necessary to align more closely with the needs and aspirations of South Africa's youth. Younger leaders must be given the opportunity to take the reins and to lead the country toward a more inclusive and equitable future.

Confronting Corruption Head-On

Corruption is a cancer that eats away at the foundations of our democracy. It erodes public trust, exacerbates inequality, and deprives citizens of essential services. Yet, corruption persists, largely unchallenged by those in power.

We must demand zero tolerance for corruption, including harsher penalties and more robust mechanisms for investigating and prosecuting corrupt officials. Corrupt leaders must be removed from power and held accountable for their actions. It is time to send a clear message that corruption will no longer be tolerated in our political system.

Reimagining Democracy

South Africa's current democratic framework is insufficient for the needs of its people. It is time to reimagine what democracy could look like in this country—a democracy that goes beyond the ballot box and involves citizens more directly in decision-making processes.

We must explore radical forms of democracy, such as participatory budgeting, local councils with real power, and mechanisms for direct citizen input on major decisions. The people of South Africa must be given the tools and the power to shape their own future, rather than being relegated to the sidelines while politicians make decisions on their behalf.

Global Solidarity and Learning

South Africa's struggles are not unique. We can learn from and contribute to global movements for justice and equity. Solidarity with other nations facing similar challenges is essential for building a stronger, more just society.

South Africa should take a leadership role in global movements for social justice. We must critique the ways in which global capital influences our politics and demand greater independence from these influences. By standing in solidarity with other nations and movements, we can strengthen our own efforts and contribute to a global push for justice and equity.

Empowerment of Marginalized Communities

Political leaders must actively empower marginalized communities—whether they are rural populations, women, or the LGBTQ+ community. This means not just protecting their rights, but also empowering them economically, socially, and politically.

Leaders must work to dismantle the structures that oppress these groups. Policies must be enacted that not only ensure their rights but also actively empower them to participate fully in society. This includes addressing the systemic barriers that have historically excluded these communities from power and influence.

The Vision for a New Political Culture

We must envision a new political culture in South Africa—one that rejects the current party system, embraces independent candidates, and fosters new political movements that are truly of, by, and for the people.

This new political culture must be built on the principles of justice, equity, and transparency. It must prioritize the common good over partisan politics and personal gain. The people of South Africa must be at the center of this new political culture, with leaders who are genuinely committed to serving their needs and aspirations.

Conclusion

The current state of political leadership in South Africa demands a radical transformation. Leaders must confront the entrenched failures of the political system, prioritize the common good, and work towards creating a society where political power is used for the benefit of all citizens. This requires abandoning partisan politics, addressing corruption, and fostering a culture of transparency and accountability.

The time for change is now, and it is up to each of us to demand more from our leaders and work towards a more just and equitable society. The path forward will not be easy, but it is necessary. Together, we can build a future where political leadership genuinely serves the common good and upholds the values of justice, equity, and integrity. The stakes have never been higher, and the time for action is now.

Chapter 12: Economic Empowerment and Development

Economic empowerment and development are not merely policy imperatives but moral imperatives in the pursuit of justice and equity in South Africa. The historical wounds of apartheid and colonialism continue to bleed through the deep-seated economic disparities that stifle the majority while disproportionately enriching a privileged few. This chapter is a clarion call for radical economic transformation—a demand to dismantle the entrenched systems of economic exclusion and replace them with structures that prioritize communal prosperity, innovation, and sustainable development. The fight for economic justice must be waged on multiple fronts: through policy reform, ethical business practices, and a return to the values of self-reliance and collective empowerment that once defined African societies.

The Failure of BBBEE and the Entrenched Exclusion of the Majority

Broad-Based Black Economic Empowerment (BBBEE) was conceived as a powerful tool to address the historical injustices of economic disenfranchisement. However, its implementation has been perverted into a superficial exercise that benefits a select few while leaving the majority trapped in cycles of poverty and marginalization. Instead of fostering widespread economic participation, BBBEE has often become a mechanism for political patronage, enriching a small elite who are more interested in maintaining their status than in driving systemic change.

The Need for Genuine Economic Reform: The failure of BBBEE is a symptom of a deeper malaise within our economic system. True economic empowerment requires more than token compliance; it demands a fundamental restructuring of the economic landscape to ensure that opportunities are accessible to all, not just the well-connected. We must advocate for reforms that dismantle the barriers to entry for black South Africans, ensuring that economic benefits are distributed equitably and that the majority can participate meaningfully in the economy. This requires a shift from a focus on individual enrichment to a commitment to collective prosperity.

The Enduring Legacy of Colonialism and Apartheid

The economic disparities that plague South Africa are not accidental; they are the deliberate result of centuries of colonial and apartheid policies designed to disenfranchise black South Africans and entrench white economic power. This legacy manifests in the psychological scars of inferiority and mistrust that continue to undermine efforts at economic solidarity and self-reliance. The disruption of African economic systems by colonialism replaced thriving, self-sufficient communities with an exploitative capitalist economy that prioritizes individual gain over communal well-being.

Reclaiming Our Economic Heritage: Before the disruptions of colonialism and apartheid, African societies were characterized by vibrant economies built on principles of communal prosperity, trade, and mutual support. To reclaim our economic autonomy, we must revive these principles of self-reliance and communal prosperity. This means investing in local industries, supporting small and medium enterprises, and fostering a culture of entrepreneurship that is rooted in our traditions and values. It also means breaking free from the psychological chains of inferiority that have been imposed on us and recognizing the inherent value and potential within our communities.

The Complicity of the Black Elite in Perpetuating Economic Inequity

One of the most troubling developments in post-apartheid South Africa is the rise of a black elite that has aligned itself with the structures of economic power, often at the expense of the broader community. Rather than using their positions to drive systemic change, many in this elite have chosen to perpetuate the very inequalities they once sought to dismantle. This self-serving approach is particularly evident in the phenomenon of tenderpreneurship, where individuals secure lucrative government contracts without delivering tangible value or creating innovative economic drivers.

The Monster of Tenderpreneurship: Tenderpreneurship has become a cancer within our economic system, elevating those who access government tenders through political connections rather than through merit or innovation. This practice not only drains public resources but also stifles genuine entrepreneurship and economic development. Instead of fostering a culture of innovation and problem-solving, tenderpreneurship promotes a parasitic relationship with the state, where wealth is extracted without contributing to the broader economy. To combat this, we must demand greater transparency and accountability in the awarding of government contracts and prioritize initiatives that support genuine entrepreneurs who create jobs, drive innovation, and contribute to societal development.

The Role of Education in Economic Disempowerment

The quality of education in our post-school education and training (PSET) institutions plays a critical role in shaping the economic landscape of South

Africa. Unfortunately, many of these institutions produce graduates who are ill-equipped to drive economic transformation. Instead of nurturing innovative thinkers and entrepreneurs, our education system often churns out employees who are trained to fit into existing structures rather than challenge them. This failure to cultivate a spirit of innovation and entrepreneurship is a significant barrier to economic empowerment.

The Crisis in Educational Output: The focus of many PSET institutions on producing employees rather than innovators is a reflection of a deeper crisis within our education system. Our institutions should be the breeding grounds for the next generation of economic leaders—individuals who can think critically, innovate, and create solutions to the pressing problems of inequality, poverty, and unemployment. Instead, we are producing graduates who are often ill-prepared to navigate the complexities of the modern economy, let alone drive the radical economic transformation that our country so desperately needs. To address this, we must overhaul our education system to prioritize skills development, critical thinking, and entrepreneurial training. We must also foster partnerships between educational institutions and the private sector to ensure that our graduates are equipped with the knowledge and skills needed to thrive in a rapidly changing economic landscape.

People-Driven Economic Transformation: Reviving Communal Prosperity

The over-reliance on formal employment as the primary means of economic participation is a departure from the self-reliant, communal economic systems that once flourished in Africa. Pre-colonial African societies were characterized by vibrant economies based on farming, trading, and communal support. These systems were disrupted by colonialism, which imposed a capitalist economy that prioritized individual gain over communal well-being.

Rebuilding Communal Economic Hubs: To reclaim our economic autonomy, we must return to these principles of communal prosperity. This means creating economic hubs within communities where local businesses can thrive, resources are shared, and collective growth is prioritized. These hubs would serve as centers for education, trade, and innovation, providing the infrastructure needed to support sustainable economic development. By fostering a spirit of cooperation and mutual support, we can create an economy that is resilient, inclusive, and rooted in the values of our heritage.

The Dilemma of Raw Material Exportation and the Need for Local Value Addition

South Africa, like much of Africa, continues to be a source of raw materials for the global economy, with little value added locally. This pattern of extraction without development not only deprives the country of potential jobs and revenue but also perpetuates a cycle of dependency on foreign markets. The wealth of our nation is being siphoned off, leaving us with little more than the crumbs of the global economy.

Investing in Local Industries for Economic Sovereignty: To break this cycle, we must invest in local industries that can process raw materials and create finished goods. This would not only keep wealth within our borders but also create jobs, foster innovation, and build economic sovereignty. We need a radical shift in our economic policy that prioritizes local production, supports small and medium enterprises, and encourages entrepreneurship. By adding value to our resources locally, we can build a stronger, more resilient economy that serves the needs of all South Africans.

Confronting Greed: The Red Ocean vs. Blue Ocean Mindset

The "Red Ocean" mindset, where individuals and companies compete in overcrowded markets, often leads to cutthroat competition, exploitation, and the hoarding of resources. This approach is driven by greed and a zero-sum mentality that sees economic success as a finite resource to be fought over rather than shared. The result is a fragmented economy where the rich get richer while the majority are left to scramble for the scraps.

Embracing the Blue Ocean Strategy: To break free from this destructive cycle, we must embrace the principles of the Blue Ocean Strategy, as articulated by Chan Kim and Renée Mauborgne. This strategy encourages the creation of new markets, where competition is irrelevant, and value is created through innovation and collaboration. By shifting our focus from competition to cooperation, we can build an economy that benefits everyone, not just the privileged few. This approach requires a radical rethinking of how we do business, placing communal growth and shared prosperity at the center of our economic activities.

The Game of Maximize Your Gain: A Lesson in Collective Prosperity

In discussions about communal prosperity and integrity, I often use a game called "Maximize Your Gain" to illustrate the importance of collective success. In this game, participants are given the choice to focus on their individual gain or work together to maximize the group's benefit. Time and again, I have seen how the lure of individual gain leads to short-term success but ultimately results in collective failure. However, when participants choose to collaborate, the rewards are far greater, demonstrating the power of communal effort in achieving prosperity.

The Role of Money in Hindering Genuine Economic Transformation

One of the most significant barriers to genuine economic transformation in South Africa is the pervasive role of money in politics and business. Financial power has come to dominate every facet of governance and economic decision-making, often to the detriment of the public good. The influence of money in politics skews policy priorities, distorts the democratic process, and reinforces economic disparities by ensuring that the wealthy and well-connected continue to benefit at the expense of the majority.

The Corruption of Capital in Political and Economic Spaces: Throughout my career, I have observed how the election of leaders and the direction of policies are increasingly determined by financial interests rather than the needs and aspirations of the people. This corrupting influence of capital ensures that those with money can manipulate the system to their advantage, creating policies that serve their interests while the majority remains marginalized. This dynamic undermines genuine economic transformation by prioritizing short-term financial gains over long-term, inclusive development. To address this issue, we must advocate for greater transparency and accountability in political and economic decision-making and challenge the entrenched power of money in our society.

Conclusion: A Call to Radical Economic Transformation

The challenges facing South Africa's economy are profound, but they are not insurmountable. By embracing a radical, people-driven approach to economic transformation, we can build a future where prosperity is shared, innovation is celebrated, and every South African has the opportunity to thrive. This requires a collective commitment to dismantling the legacy of colonialism and apartheid, confronting the corrosive influence of money in politics and business, and fostering a culture of integrity, collaboration, and communal prosperity.

The time for change is now. The responsibility lies with each of us to demand and create the economic transformation that our country so desperately needs. By rejecting the status quo and embracing a vision of shared prosperity, we can build an economy that works for everyone, not just the privileged few. The journey towards economic empowerment and development will not be easy, but it is a journey that we must undertake if we are to create a just and equitable society for all South Africans.

Chapter 13: Education as a Catalyst for Change

Education is not merely a tool for personal advancement; it is the very foundation upon which societal transformation is built. In South Africa, where the shadows of historical injustices still loom large, our educational system must be radically reimagined to become a true catalyst for change. This chapter challenges us to view education not as a passive conveyor of outdated knowledge but as an active engine for societal revolution. The imperative is clear: education must be redesigned to address our deepest societal needs, foster innovation, and drive equitable progress. This call is anchored in a vision of education that aligns with the core values expressed in *Unmute Courageous Catalysts: Leading South Africa Beyond Historical Trauma and Fragmentation*.

The Current Crisis in Education

The educational system in South Africa is in crisis. It is failing to equip students with the skills necessary to thrive in the 21st century. The curriculum remains mired in outdated practices that prioritize rote memorization over critical thinking, real-world application, and problem-solving. This disconnection between what is taught and what is needed in the real world is not just a failing; it is a perpetuation of the systemic inequities that have long plagued our society. I have witnessed firsthand the disillusionment of students graduating from institutions with degrees that do not translate into meaningful opportunities. This reality is not only heartbreaking but also a betrayal of the promises that education should deliver.

Technological Integration and Digital Literacy

In an era where technology is rapidly transforming every aspect of life, our education system must keep pace. Integrating technology into the curriculum is no longer optional—it is essential. Digital literacy should be embedded across all subjects, preparing students not just to use technology, but to critically engage with it. This involves teaching students to navigate the digital landscape, discern credible information from misinformation, and use technology as a tool for innovation and problem-solving. As we move deeper into the digital age, failing to equip our students with these skills is equivalent to setting them up for failure in the global economy.

Education and the Biblical Call for Transformation

From a biblical perspective, education is not just about acquiring knowledge but about seeking wisdom and understanding that lead to justice and righteousness. Proverbs 4:7 urges us to "Get wisdom. Though it cost all you have, get understanding." This call to seek wisdom underscores the transformative potential of education. Education should be a conduit for divine justice, equipping individuals to challenge injustices and seek the common good. It should be a powerful tool for moral and ethical growth, ensuring that our educational practices contribute to a just and equitable world.

The Challenge of Educational Reform

Addressing the crisis in education requires confronting several critical issues:

1. **Redesigning the Curriculum:**
   Our current curriculum is a relic of a bygone era, failing to reflect the needs of today's students. It is time to overhaul this curriculum to include practical skills, critical thinking, and an understanding of contemporary social and economic issues. Integrating lessons on entrepreneurship, civic responsibility, and social justice into the core curriculum will prepare students to tackle real-world problems and drive innovation.
2. **Empowering Teachers:**
   Teachers are at the frontline of educational transformation. They need to be supported with resources, training, and autonomy to foster creativity, critical thinking, and social consciousness in their students. Investing in teacher development is not just about improving teaching methods but about transforming the educational experience for students.
3. **Community and Parental Engagement:**
   Education is not an isolated endeavor. It thrives on the active involvement of parents, communities, and faith leaders. Schools must work in partnership with families and community organizations to create supportive learning environments and address local needs.
4. **Fostering Innovation and Leadership:**
   We need to create educational environments that nurture leadership and innovation. Students should be encouraged to take on leadership roles and engage in projects that drive community development and social change. This involves creating platforms where students can explore their passions and apply their skills meaningfully.
5. **Aligning Education with Economic Needs:**
   There must be a clear link between education and economic opportunities. Integrating vocational training, apprenticeships, and industry partnerships into the educational system will ensure that

students are prepared for meaningful employment and can contribute to economic growth.

6. **Addressing Historical Inequities:**
   The education system must actively work to address historical injustices. This involves implementing policies that ensure equal access to quality education for all students, particularly those from historically marginalized communities. Confronting and dismantling systemic barriers is essential to creating an equitable educational landscape.

7. **Mental Health and Well-being in Education:**
   The pressures of modern education, coupled with societal challenges, significantly impact the mental health and well-being of students. Educational institutions must prioritize mental health by providing resources and support systems that address these challenges. A healthy mind is critical for academic success and personal development, and this must be recognized as a cornerstone of educational reform.

8. **Equitable Resource Allocation:**
   Disparities in resource allocation across schools, particularly between urban and rural areas, are a major barrier to quality education. Policies must ensure that all schools have access to the resources they need to provide quality education. This includes infrastructure, teaching materials, and technological tools that are essential for creating an effective learning environment.

9. **Lifelong Learning and Continuing Education:**
   Education should not end with formal schooling but should be an ongoing process that allows individuals to adapt to changes in the job market and society. Promoting lifelong learning opportunities, such as adult education and professional development programs, is essential for maintaining a dynamic and responsive workforce.

10. **Confronting Misguided Curricula:**
    The current curricula in many schools are misguided and fail to address the real needs of students. They perpetuate a Eurocentric view of knowledge that marginalizes diverse cultures. This approach alienates students and reinforces exclusion and inequality. We must advocate for curricula that are inclusive and reflective of our society's diversity. This means integrating local histories, languages, and perspectives into the educational framework, ensuring that education is relevant and equitable for all students.

The Role of Faith Leaders and Community Stakeholders

Faith leaders and community stakeholders have a pivotal role in transforming education. They must advocate for and support educational reforms that align with values of justice and equity. This involves not only challenging existing norms but also creating new platforms for educational engagement. Faith communities and local organizations must work together to drive initiatives that address educational inequities and foster a culture of learning and growth.

The Moral Imperative for Educational Leadership

Educational leaders must recognize their role as agents of change. They are not merely administrators but visionaries who must lead with conviction and challenge the status quo. This involves advocating for policies that promote equitable access to quality education and confronting entrenched interests that resist change. Ethical leadership in education is about more than managing institutions; it is about transforming them into forces for societal progress.

Practical Steps for Transformation

To drive meaningful educational reform, the following practical steps must be taken:

1. **Advocate for Curriculum Reform:**
   Engage with policymakers and educational leaders to push for curriculum changes that reflect contemporary needs and values. Support initiatives that promote critical thinking, social responsibility, and real-world application.
2. **Invest in Teacher Training:**
   Support programs that provide teachers with the skills and resources needed to implement innovative teaching methods. Encourage ongoing professional development and create opportunities for teachers to share best practices.
3. **Foster Community Partnerships:**
   Build strong partnerships between schools, families, and community organizations. Create platforms for collaboration and ensure that educational initiatives are responsive to local needs.
4. **Promote Inclusivity:**
   Advocate for educational practices that reflect the diverse backgrounds and experiences of students. Ensure that curricula and teaching methods are inclusive and equitable.
5. **Align Education with Economic Needs:**
   Develop partnerships between educational institutions and industry to ensure that curricula are aligned with workforce demands. Promote vocational training and apprenticeships as viable pathways to employment.

6. **Address Historical Inequities:**
   Implement policies that address historical injustices and promote equal access to quality education. Work to dismantle systemic barriers and create opportunities for marginalized communities.
7. **Encourage Civic Engagement:**
   Promote civic education and encourage students to engage in community service and social activism. Foster a sense of responsibility and commitment to societal change.

Call to Action and Conclusion

The title of this book, *Unmute Courageous Catalysts: Leading South Africa Beyond Historical Trauma and Fragmentation*, captures the essence of the radical change required in our educational system. The principles outlined within these pages demand an educational revolution that aligns with the vision of a transformed society. Education must become a powerful vehicle for justice, innovation, and societal progress.

The current education system, with its outdated curricula and rote memorization methods, fails to serve the needs of our society effectively. As I have witnessed in various academic institutions, the "tick-the-box" mindset dominates, overshadowing genuine understanding and practical application. Despite facilitating numerous strategic planning sessions, I have encountered a troubling resistance to unlearning entrenched practices in favor of progressive and innovative approaches. The high levels of graduate unemployment starkly highlight the deficiencies in critical thinking and practical readiness produced by our institutions.

In response to this, I have initiated the Unmuting Confidence wing within Lindbong Development. This program is designed to help graduates and individuals in the post-schooling phase rediscover themselves, embrace their realities, and articulate their aspirations with confidence. It reflects Alvin Toffler's insight that "the illiterate of the twenty-first century is not those who cannot read and write but those who cannot unlearn, relearn, and learn." This perspective is crucial for understanding that education must be dynamic and responsive, not static and antiquated.

The time for incremental change is over. We need a radical overhaul of our educational approach to ensure it serves as a true catalyst for societal transformation. This involves not just reforming curricula but also embracing innovative teaching methods, fostering community engagement, and addressing historical inequities. Every stakeholder, from academic leaders to parents, must commit to creating an educational system that empowers all South Africans to contribute meaningfully to our collective future.

We must confront the painful reality of our current educational system with urgency and determination. The future of our nation depends on an education system that not only prepares students for the present but also equips them to shape a better tomorrow. Let us rise to this challenge and build an educational framework that truly serves the common good, transforming our society and advancing the cause of justice and equity for all.

Chapter 14: Building Trust and Accountability

Trust and accountability are the bedrock of cohesive societies, effective governance, and sustainable development. Without these foundational elements, any efforts towards transformation and growth are destined to crumble. In the context of South Africa's tumultuous past and challenging present, fostering trust and accountability is more critical than ever. This chapter draws from Dennis Peacocke's writings on restoring the bridge of trust and weaves them into a broader narrative that considers our historical context, current realities, and the themes that drive this book.

Restoring the Bridge of Trust

Dennis Peacocke emphasizes the necessity of restoring trust as a fundamental step toward societal healing and progress. Trust is not merely a desirable quality but an essential component of any functional relationship, be it between individuals, communities, or institutions. In South Africa, the legacy of apartheid has left deep scars, eroding trust across racial, social, and economic lines. Rebuilding this trust requires intentional, sustained efforts to address past injustices, foster open dialogue, and promote transparency.

Peacocke's concept of "restoring the bridge of trust" involves several key principles: honesty, transparency, consistency, and relational investment. Trust cannot be demanded; it must be earned through actions that demonstrate reliability and integrity. This is especially pertinent in a society like ours, where mistrust has been institutionalized through decades of systemic oppression and corruption.

Historical Context and the Erosion of Trust

The systematic erosion of trust in South Africa has deep roots in the country's history of colonialism and apartheid. These eras were characterized by the deliberate manipulation and control of information, the entrenchment of inequality, and the brutal suppression of dissent. Communities were pitted against each other, and trust in institutions was systematically dismantled. This historical backdrop makes the task of rebuilding trust all the more daunting but also all the more necessary.

The Truth and Reconciliation Commission (TRC), while a monumental step in addressing some of these issues, also highlighted the deep-seated mistrust that lingers in South African society. Many felt that the TRC was more focused on truth-telling than on ensuring justice and reparation, leaving wounds only partially healed. This context underscores the need for a renewed commitment to trust-building that goes beyond surface-level reconciliation.

Biblical Frameworks for Trust and Accountability

The Bible provides profound insights into the importance of trust and accountability. Proverbs 22:1 states, "A good name is more desirable than great riches; to be esteemed is better than silver or gold." This scripture highlights the intrinsic value of trustworthiness and the long-term benefits it brings, surpassing even material wealth. Trust is foundational to all relationships and endeavors; without it, any achievements are superficial and unsustainable.

Furthermore, the principle of accountability is deeply embedded in biblical teachings. Galatians 6:7 reminds us that "a man reaps what he sows." This principle underscores the importance of being accountable for one's actions, understanding that our choices have consequences that affect not only ourselves but also those around us. In fostering trust, we must hold ourselves and others accountable, ensuring that actions align with words and commitments.

Personal Experience and Insights

Throughout my career, I have consistently witnessed the critical role of trust and accountability in achieving meaningful progress. While servicing various academic institutions, I have seen the detrimental effects of a "tick-the-box" mindset driven by assessment outcomes over quality understanding and practical application in the broader market and societal space. During strategic planning sessions, I have discovered that some academics resist unlearning outdated methods to embrace progressive and innovative measures. The level of graduate unemployment is a testament to the poor quality of critical thinking produced by our institutions.

I have facilitated numerous strategic planning sessions and found that many academics are not open to unlearning old ways to embrace progressive and innovative measures. This resistance hampers the development of critical thinking and practical skills in graduates, contributing to high unemployment rates. To address this, I introduced a wing within Lindbong Development called "Unmuting Confidence." This initiative helps graduates and those in the post-schooling phase to discover themselves, embrace their reality, appreciate who they are becoming, and articulate their dreams, mission, and pursuit of life with great confidence.

In my work, I have always emphasized the importance of impartiality over neutrality. Whenever I facilitate an election or mediation process, I make it clear that I do not subscribe to neutrality but am a firm believer and implementer of impartiality. This conviction has earned me the trust of political parties, corporations, and other stakeholders. By consistently demonstrating integrity and impartiality, I have built a reputation that underscores the power of trust in fostering collaboration and achieving common goals.

I have witnessed how easily trust can be broken and how integrity can produce more trust and earn you more credibility. I took a decision early in my life that I would rather suffer the consequences of being on the side of truth than build my life and personal dreams on things that would compromise my integrity and people's trust in me and the work I do. When I entered the business world, I was shocked at how many opportunities I kept losing and missing because I refused to pay bribes or allow the manipulation of processes. Over the years, I found myself rated among the most trusted service providers in elections management, alternative dispute resolutions, and mediation. This was because I built my own credibility and protected myself from being co-opted into the world of shortcuts and easy wins. I became more accountable, more credible, and subsequently more trustworthy. Building trust is not an easy task, but it is a fulfilling one.

The Role of Trust and Accountability in Transformation

Trust and accountability are not just moral imperatives; they are practical necessities for societal transformation. They provide the foundation upon which diverse groups can collaborate effectively. When trust is established, individuals and organizations are more willing to engage openly, share resources, and work towards common objectives. Accountability ensures that these efforts are aligned with ethical standards and collective goals, preventing the misuse of power and resources.

Proximity brings clarity; trust emerges from clarity and intentional interface as unity develops at the speed of trust. This principle is crucial for transforming South African society. By fostering close, transparent relationships, we can overcome historical divisions and build a united front for progress. Trust facilitates collaboration, while accountability ensures that these collaborations are fruitful and sustainable.

Challenges in Building Trust and Accountability

Building trust and accountability in South Africa faces numerous challenges:

- **Historical Mistrust**: Overcoming the deep-seated mistrust bred by decades of apartheid and colonial rule requires sustained, intentional efforts to address past wrongs and promote justice.
- **Corruption and Nepotism**: The pervasive culture of corruption and nepotism in both public and private sectors severely undermines trust. This requires not just policies but a cultural shift towards ethical behavior and integrity.
- **Political Manipulation**: Trust is further eroded by political leaders who manipulate information and processes for personal or partisan gain. This has led to widespread cynicism and disengagement among the public.

Practical Benefits of Building Trust and Accountability

For individuals, building trust and accountability leads to stronger relationships, enhanced reputations, and greater personal fulfillment. Trustworthy individuals are more likely to be entrusted with responsibilities and opportunities, creating a virtuous cycle of growth and success. For organizations, these principles foster a positive culture, enhance employee engagement, and drive sustainable success. Organizations that prioritize trust and accountability tend to attract and retain top talent, build loyal customer bases, and achieve long-term stability.

The Role of Technology in Trust and Accountability

In today's digital age, technology plays a dual role in trust and accountability. On one hand, digital platforms can enhance transparency by providing easy access to information, facilitating communication, and enabling public oversight. On the other hand, the same technologies can be used to spread misinformation, manipulate public opinion, and erode trust. Balancing these potentials requires a commitment to ethical use of technology and the promotion of digital literacy among the population.

Case Studies and Global Perspectives

Examples from around the world show that rebuilding trust and accountability is possible even in deeply divided societies. The post-war reconciliation efforts in Germany, Rwanda's approach to community-based justice (Gacaca courts), and New Zealand's Truth and Reconciliation processes with the Maori people all offer valuable lessons. These case studies illustrate that while the path to rebuilding trust is complex and often fraught with setbacks, sustained commitment to transparency, justice, and ethical leadership can lead to profound societal transformation.

Practical Steps for Fostering Trust and Accountability

1. **Promote Transparency**: Transparency is the cornerstone of trust. Organizations and leaders must prioritize open communication, sharing information honestly and openly with all stakeholders. This includes being forthright about challenges and setbacks, as well as successes.
2. **Encourage Ethical Behavior**: Establishing and enforcing clear ethical standards is essential for accountability. This involves creating codes of conduct, providing ethics training, and implementing robust mechanisms for reporting and addressing unethical behavior.
3. **Foster Open Dialogue**: Create platforms for open, honest dialogue where all voices can be heard. This encourages mutual understanding and trust. Regularly solicit feedback and be responsive to concerns and suggestions.
4. **Lead by Example**: Leaders must embody the principles of trust and accountability in their actions. By consistently demonstrating integrity and accountability, leaders set the standard for others to follow.
5. **Invest in Relationships**: Building trust requires relational investment. Spend time cultivating relationships with stakeholders, understanding their needs, and demonstrating a genuine commitment to their well-being.
6. **Implement Accountability Mechanisms**: Establish clear accountability structures to ensure that actions align with commitments. This includes regular performance reviews, transparent reporting processes, and consequences for breaches of trust.
7. **Promote Collaborative Efforts**: Encourage collaboration across diverse groups. Trust is built through shared experiences and collaborative successes. Facilitate partnerships and joint initiatives that promote mutual goals.

Call to Action and Conclusion

Trust and accountability are not optional in this journey; they are essential. We must commit to these principles in all spheres of society—academic, political, corporate, and community. Our collective future depends on our ability to build and sustain trust, to hold ourselves and others accountable, and to work together towards a just and equitable society.

As South Africans, we face a unique historical and social landscape that demands radical, compassionate, and action-driven leadership. By embracing the principles of trust and accountability, we can bridge historical divides, foster unity, and drive transformative change. Let us commit to this journey with integrity and conviction, unmuting our potential as courageous catalysts for a better future.

Chapter 15: Promoting Mental Health and Well-being

In our pursuit to lead South Africa beyond historical trauma and fragmentation, the mental health and well-being of our leaders are paramount. The mission of "Unmute Courageous Catalysts" demands resilience, clarity, and sustained passion. To achieve this, we must address the mental health of those at the forefront of our transformative journey. This chapter explores the significance of mental health for leaders, the challenges they face, and practical steps to foster well-being and resilience.

The Impact of Mental Health on Leadership

Leaders are the driving force behind societal change. They are tasked with shaping lives, making critical decisions, and navigating complex challenges. However, the immense pressure and responsibility that come with leadership can take a significant toll on their mental health. The effects of stress, burnout, and emotional fatigue are profound, impacting not only the leaders themselves but also the people they serve.

In my journey, I have witnessed the emotional and psychological strain that leaders endure. The frustration of encountering resistance, the burden of high expectations, and the relentless pursuit of transformative change can lead to burnout, depression, and a decline in overall well-being. The frustration encountered in the attempts to transform the nation is often overwhelming, and the mental health of leaders must be prioritized to sustain this mission.

Promoting Mental Health Among Leaders

To sustain the mission of unmuting courageous catalysts and leading our nation beyond historical trauma, leaders must prioritize their mental health and personal well-being. This involves several key practices:

1. **Debriefing and Self-Care:** Regular debriefing sessions provide leaders with an opportunity to reflect, process their experiences, and release built-up stress. Self-care practices, such as exercise, meditation, and hobbies, are vital for maintaining mental and emotional health.
2. **Seeking Support:** Leaders should not hesitate to seek support from mental health professionals, mentors, and peers. Counseling, therapy, and support groups offer a safe space to discuss challenges and receive guidance.
3. **Rest and Sabbath:** Embracing the principle of rest and Sabbath is crucial for rejuvenation. Taking regular breaks, honoring rest days, and

disconnecting from work-related stressors can prevent burnout and enhance well-being. The Bible underscores the importance of rest, as seen in Exodus 20:8-10, where the Sabbath is instituted as a day of rest and worship.

4. **Healthy Work-Life Balance:** Establishing a healthy work-life balance is essential. Leaders should set boundaries between work and personal life, ensuring they allocate time for family, relaxation, and self-care.
5. **Resilience Training:** Engaging in resilience training programs equips leaders with tools to cope with stress, adapt to challenges, and maintain a positive outlook. Resilience is not just about bouncing back but also about growing through adversity.
6. **Journaling and Reflection:** Keeping a journal can help leaders process their thoughts and emotions, offering a space to reflect on their experiences and gain insights into their mental and emotional state. Regular reflection can lead to greater self-awareness and emotional clarity.
7. **Gratitude Practice:** Practicing gratitude can shift the focus from stress and challenges to positive aspects of life and work. Regularly expressing gratitude can improve mental well-being and foster a more optimistic outlook.
8. **Mindfulness and Meditation:** Incorporating mindfulness and meditation practices can help leaders stay grounded and present, reducing anxiety and enhancing emotional regulation. These practices are powerful tools for managing stress and maintaining mental clarity.

The Role of Mental Health in Transformative Leadership

Transforming a nation requires leaders who are mentally and emotionally healthy. Leaders who neglect their mental health may struggle with decision-making, experience decreased productivity, and become disengaged from their mission. Moreover, leaders who are not attuned to their own well-being may inadvertently project their stress and frustration onto their teams, creating a toxic work environment.

As leaders, we must recognize the importance of mental health in fulfilling our roles effectively. Promoting mental health among leaders has far-reaching implications, including:

1. **Enhanced Decision-Making:** Mentally healthy leaders are better equipped to make sound, strategic decisions. They can think clearly, remain calm under pressure, and approach problems with creativity and insight.

2. **Increased Productivity:** Leaders who prioritize their well-being are more productive and efficient. They have the energy and focus needed to drive initiatives forward and inspire their teams.
3. **Improved Relationships:** Mental health influences how leaders interact with others. Leaders who are emotionally balanced can build stronger, more positive relationships with colleagues, stakeholders, and the community.
4. **Sustainable Leadership:** By taking care of their mental health, leaders can sustain their passion and commitment to their mission over the long term. They are less likely to experience burnout and can continue to lead with enthusiasm and purpose.

The Vulnerability of Transformational Leaders

Transformational leaders, by their very nature, are often on the front lines of social and political change. This exposes them to unique challenges, including opposition, criticism, and, at times, outright hostility. The emotional toll of such resistance can be immense, leading to feelings of isolation, frustration, and self-doubt. It's crucial for these leaders to recognize that vulnerability is not a weakness but a testament to their deep commitment to their cause.

Drawing from the animated movie "Inside Out," we can see how different emotions—joy, sadness, fear, anger, and disgust—play vital roles in shaping our experiences and responses to challenges. Leaders must acknowledge and embrace their full range of emotions, understanding that each one has a purpose in their leadership journey. By doing so, they can maintain emotional balance and resilience in the face of adversity.

Addressing Burnout and Fatigue

Burnout and fatigue are significant threats to leaders' mental health. The constant demands of leadership, coupled with the pressure to achieve transformative outcomes, can lead to exhaustion and a sense of overwhelm. To address burnout and fatigue, leaders should:

1. **Recognize the Signs:** Leaders must be aware of the signs of burnout, such as chronic fatigue, irritability, decreased motivation, and emotional detachment. Early recognition allows for timely intervention.
2. **Practice Mindfulness:** Mindfulness practices, such as meditation and deep breathing exercises, help leaders stay present and manage stress. Mindfulness can improve emotional regulation and enhance overall well-being.

3. **Delegate Responsibilities:** Leaders should delegate tasks to trusted team members to reduce their workload. Effective delegation empowers others and ensures that leaders are not overburdened.
4. **Set Realistic Goals:** Setting realistic, achievable goals prevents leaders from becoming overwhelmed. Break down larger objectives into manageable steps and celebrate progress along the way.
5. **Create Supportive Environments:** Fostering a culture of support within organizations and communities encourages open communication and mutual assistance. Leaders should cultivate environments where team members feel valued and supported.

Scriptural Guidance for Mental Health and Well-being

Scripture offers profound insights into the importance of mental health and well-being. For instance, in **Philippians 4:6-7**, Paul advises, "Do not be anxious about anything, but in every situation, by prayer and petition, with thanksgiving, present your requests to God. And the peace of God, which transcends all understanding, will guard your hearts and your minds in Christ Jesus." This passage underscores the importance of spiritual practices like prayer and gratitude in maintaining mental peace and emotional stability.

Similarly, **Matthew 11:28-30** invites us to find rest in Christ: "Come to me, all you who are weary and burdened, and I will give you rest. Take my yoke upon you and learn from me, for I am gentle and humble in heart, and you will find rest for your souls. For my yoke is easy and my burden is light." This scripture emphasizes the importance of rest and the need to lean on spiritual strength during times of stress and burden.

Personal Experience and Insights

I have learned that no matter how severe the process I am engaging in—whether in mediation, social engagement, facilitating an election, or any part of my work—I prioritize my personal well-being. I intentionally pull back and allow my head and heart to breathe before serving people and their needs more. I have sadly experienced burnout before, and it is the most painful and frustrating experience, especially when it hits you at the prime of your engagements and activities as a leader.

Through these experiences, I have come to understand the critical importance of maintaining my mental health. The decision to prioritize well-being, even in the face of pressing demands, is not just a matter of personal preservation but a strategic choice that enables me to serve more effectively. Building in regular practices of rest, reflection, and self-care has become essential to sustaining my leadership and continuing the transformative work I am committed to.

Conclusion

Promoting mental health and well-being among leaders is essential for achieving the transformative goals outlined in "Unmute Courageous Catalysts." By prioritizing mental health, leaders can enhance their decision-making, productivity, relationships, and resilience. Embracing practices such as debriefing, seeking support, maintaining a work-life balance, and addressing burnout will enable leaders to sustain their passion and commitment to their mission. By fostering a culture of trust and accountability, leaders can inspire others and create a positive impact on the communities they serve.

Let us prioritize mental health and well-being as we lead South Africa beyond historical trauma and fragmentation, unmuting the courageous catalysts who will shape a brighter future for our nation.

Chapter 16: Navigating Cultural Sensitivities

In the complex and vibrant tapestry of South Africa, navigating cultural sensitivities is not just a leadership skill—it's a moral imperative. As we endeavor to lead South Africa beyond its historical traumas and persistent divisions, the ability to engage with cultural diversity is crucial. This chapter will not only explore the depths of cultural sensitivities but also challenge you, as a leader and catalyst for change, to radically embrace and champion the richness of our nation's diverse cultural heritage. In doing so, we must confront the systemic barriers, biases, and prejudices that have long impeded our progress, ensuring that our leadership is as inclusive and transformative as the vision we espouse.

The Heart of Cultural Sensitivity

Understanding Cultural Diversity

South Africa's cultural landscape is as vast and varied as its geography. The nation's diversity is its greatest strength, yet it also presents significant challenges for leaders who seek to unify people across cultural lines. Understanding and honoring this diversity is not optional—it is a prerequisite for effective leadership in a nation still grappling with the legacies of apartheid and colonialism. Every cultural group within South Africa carries a history, a legacy, and a unique set of values that must be respected and understood.

But understanding cultural diversity goes beyond simple acknowledgment. It requires a deep and sincere engagement with the lived experiences of others. Leaders must immerse themselves in the cultural narratives of the people they lead, recognizing that these narratives are not just peripheral stories but central elements of identity. It is through this engagement that we can begin to dismantle the systemic inequalities that continue to marginalize certain groups and build a truly inclusive society.

Cultural sensitivity is about more than just avoiding offense—it's about actively promoting dignity, respect, and equity. It's about challenging the ingrained prejudices that have historically placed one culture above another and ensuring that all cultural expressions are valued and celebrated.

Personal Experiences and Reflections

My journey as a social engagement facilitator and transformation agent has brought me face to face with the deep cultural divides that exist in our nation. I've seen how easily misunderstandings can arise, not out of malice but out of ignorance. However, I've also witnessed the incredible power of cultural sensitivity to bridge these divides, creating spaces where genuine dialogue and mutual respect can flourish.

One of the most profound lessons I've learned is that cultural sensitivity is not a static skill—it is a dynamic, ongoing process. In one of the communities I worked with, which had a rich cultural heritage rooted in deep traditions, I was initially an outsider. I knew that to be effective, I needed to gain their trust, and the only way to do that was by fully immersing myself in their cultural practices. I spent time listening, learning, and participating in their rituals. This investment of time and effort not only built trust but also opened up avenues for deeper collaboration and more meaningful outcomes.

In another scenario, working with a diverse group of youth, I encountered the challenges of navigating multiple cultural perspectives simultaneously. Each participant came with their own set of cultural norms and expectations. The success of our work depended on creating a space where all these perspectives could coexist and where every participant felt their voice was heard and valued. This was not just about facilitating dialogue—it was about fostering a culture of mutual respect and empathy that could transcend cultural boundaries.

Through these experiences, I have come to understand that cultural sensitivity is a form of leadership that requires humility, openness, and a willingness to learn. It is not enough to be aware of cultural differences; we must actively seek to understand them, engage with them, and, where necessary, challenge the systemic structures that perpetuate cultural hierarchies.

Principles for Navigating Cultural Sensitivities

1. **Radical Active Listening and Empathy**
    - Active listening is not just a technique; it is a radical act of solidarity with those whose voices have historically been marginalized. It requires us to listen not just with our ears but with our hearts, to truly hear the pain, the joy, the struggles, and the triumphs of those from different cultural backgrounds. Empathy, in this context, is not a passive feeling but an active engagement with the lived realities of others. It demands that we step outside of our own cultural frameworks and see the world through the eyes of others.

- **Scriptural Insight**: James 1:19 is a call to action: "Everyone should be quick to listen, slow to speak and slow to become angry." This verse is a powerful reminder that leadership grounded in cultural sensitivity starts with the willingness to listen first and foremost.

2. **Uncompromising Respect for Traditions and Beliefs**
    - Respect is more than tolerance—it is a deep recognition of the inherent worth of all cultural practices, even those that challenge our own beliefs. As leaders, we must be willing to adapt our methods and approaches to align with the cultural norms of the communities we serve. This respect must be uncompromising, even when it is inconvenient or uncomfortable. It requires us to confront our own biases and to dismantle any remnants of cultural superiority that may linger in our attitudes or practices.
    - **Scriptural Insight**: 1 Peter 2:17 commands us to "Show proper respect to everyone." This directive is non-negotiable in our efforts to build an inclusive society.

3. **Courageous Open Dialogue and Collaboration**
    - Open dialogue is the foundation of cultural sensitivity, but it must be courageous dialogue—conversations that are willing to tackle the difficult and uncomfortable issues that arise from cultural differences. Collaboration across cultural lines is not just a strategy; it is a necessity. In fostering these dialogues, we must ensure that every voice is given equal weight and that no cultural perspective is dismissed or diminished. Collaboration must be rooted in a mutual respect that acknowledges the value of each participant's cultural background.
    - **Scriptural Insight**: Proverbs 27:17 reminds us that "As iron sharpens iron, so one person sharpens another." This highlights the transformative power of collaboration when it is grounded in respect and mutual benefit.

4. **Relentlessly Addressing Cultural Misunderstandings**
    - Cultural misunderstandings are not just obstacles to be overcome; they are opportunities for growth and learning. When they occur, they must be addressed head-on, with a relentless commitment to clarity and understanding. This requires humility, the willingness to admit when we are wrong, and the courage to seek reconciliation. Misunderstandings, when handled with care and respect, can actually deepen trust and strengthen relationships.
    - **Scriptural Insight**: Matthew 5:24 emphasizes the importance of reconciliation: "Leave your gift there in front of the altar. First go and be reconciled to them; then come and offer your gift." This

underscores the need for prompt and genuine efforts to resolve cultural misunderstandings.

5. **Integrating Kingdom Values with Boldness**
   - Integrating Kingdom values into our leadership practices is not just about being ethical—it is about being radically counter-cultural in a world that often prioritizes power over people. Kingdom values such as love, humility, and justice must be the bedrock upon which we build our cultural sensitivity. These values call us to love our neighbors as ourselves, to seek justice for the oppressed, and to walk humbly with our God. They challenge us to create spaces where all individuals are valued and where cultural diversity is celebrated as a reflection of God's own creative genius.
   - **Scriptural Insight**: Galatians 3:28 calls us to unity in diversity: "There is neither Jew nor Gentile, neither slave nor free, nor is there male and female, for you are all one in Christ Jesus." This verse challenges us to tear down the cultural divisions that separate us and to build a community that reflects the inclusive love of Christ.

Practical Applications

1. **Creating Culturally Inclusive Programs with Intentionality**
   - Developing culturally inclusive programs requires more than just superficial adjustments—it demands a fundamental shift in how we design and implement initiatives. Programs must be tailored to reflect the diverse needs and preferences of the communities we serve. This includes incorporating cultural practices into program activities, offering resources in multiple languages, and ensuring that program content respects and honors cultural norms and values. This is not about ticking boxes; it is about embedding cultural sensitivity into the very DNA of our programs.
2. **Transformative Training and Awareness Initiatives**
   - Providing training on cultural sensitivity and awareness must go beyond basic orientation—it must be transformative. Leaders and team members need deep, immersive training that challenges their assumptions and equips them with the skills to engage with cultural diversity at a profound level. This includes understanding the historical contexts of different cultures, developing effective communication strategies, and learning how to navigate cultural conflicts with grace and effectiveness.
3. **Engaging with Communities through Authentic Relationships**

- Authentic community engagement is the cornerstone of effective cultural sensitivity. This involves more than just consulting with cultural leaders—it requires building genuine relationships based on mutual respect and trust. Community engagement efforts should be co-created with cultural representatives, ensuring that initiatives are not only aligned with community needs but also driven by the communities themselves. This approach empowers communities and ensures that cultural sensitivity is not just a leadership practice but a community-wide ethos.
4. **Continuous Improvement through Radical Feedback**
    - Soliciting feedback from diverse cultural groups is not a one-time event—it is an ongoing process that requires radical transparency and a commitment to continuous improvement. Feedback should be actively sought, deeply considered, and swiftly acted upon. This demonstrates our commitment to cultural sensitivity and fosters ongoing trust and collaboration. Continuous improvement based on feedback is not just a practice—it is a statement of our dedication to creating a more inclusive and respectful society.

Conclusion

Navigating cultural sensitivities is not a passive process—it is an active, radical commitment to equity, justice, and inclusivity. It demands more than just knowledge—it requires a deep engagement with the lived experiences of others and a willingness to challenge the systemic structures that perpetuate cultural hierarchies. By embracing the principles of "Unmute Courageous Catalysts" and integrating Kingdom values into our leadership, we can create environments where every individual is valued and every cultural expression is honored.

As we continue to work towards building a more equitable and unified society, let us remain committed to understanding and honoring the rich cultural diversity that defines South Africa. Through active listening, respectful engagement, and a relentless commitment to continuous improvement, we can navigate cultural sensitivities with the boldness and grace that are required to lead our communities towards a more inclusive and harmonious future. Let us not just navigate cultural sensitivities—let us conquer them, transforming them from challenges into opportunities for growth, unity, and collective empowerment.

Chapter 17: Transformative Justice and Reconciliation

In the quest to heal a nation scarred by historical injustices and fractured by societal inequities, transformative justice and reconciliation stand as pillars of hope and renewal. As we navigate this complex landscape, it is crucial to forge a path towards true justice and healing, guided by Biblical principles, the values enshrined in the South African Constitution, and radical, Kingdom-minded perspectives on justice and restitution. This chapter reflects my journey as a practitioner, leader, and citizen committed to fostering transformation, reconciliation, and justice in our society.

The Imperative for Transformative Justice

Historical Context and the Need for Justice

South Africa's transition from apartheid to democracy marked a significant shift towards political freedom. However, the negotiated settlement of this transition left many crucial issues unresolved, particularly concerning justice and restitution for the deep-seated injustices of apartheid. While the Truth and Reconciliation Commission (TRC) made strides in addressing past wrongs, its approach to justice was often seen as insufficiently robust in delivering comprehensive restitution and reparations.

Reflecting on the TRC's limitations, **Prof. Mahmood Mamdani** argues, "If the point is to restore the dignity of victims, then the measure of success is not only in telling the truth but also in delivering justice... in addressing the underlying conditions that made the violence possible in the first place." This insight underscores the need for a justice system that not only acknowledges past wrongs but actively works to dismantle the systemic inequalities that continue to oppress the majority.

Similarly, **Rev. Allan Boesak** contends that, "True reconciliation cannot exist without justice, and justice must include restitution—economic, social, and psychological—if we are to move beyond the superficial peace." Boesak's call for radical reconciliation aligns with the chapter's assertion that the path to true justice must be both transformative and inclusive, addressing the root causes of disparity rather than merely treating its symptoms.

Biblical Principles of Justice and Reconciliation

The Scriptures offer profound insights into the nature of justice and reconciliation, principles that are foundational to transformative justice. In the Bible, justice is deeply intertwined with righteousness and equity, and reconciliation is depicted as a process of healing and restoration.

1. **Justice as Righteousness**: In Micah 6:8, we are instructed to "act justly and to love mercy and to walk humbly with your God." This call to justice reflects a commitment to righteousness, fairness, and the well-being of all individuals, particularly the marginalized and oppressed.
2. **Restitution and Reparations**: The concept of restitution is rooted in biblical law, as seen in Exodus 22:1, which calls for the repayment of stolen property. This principle underscores the importance of making amends for wrongs and ensuring that those who have been harmed receive justice.
3. **Reconciliation and Restoration**: The New Testament emphasizes reconciliation as a process of healing and renewal. In 2 Corinthians 5:18-19, Paul speaks of the ministry of reconciliation, highlighting the role of forgiveness and the restoration of relationships as central to the Christian faith.

As **Prof. Pumla Gobodo-Madikizela** reflects on the complexities of forgiveness within the South African context, she emphasizes that "forgiveness is not a cheap grace; it demands a deep engagement with the wounds of the past and a commitment to repair the harm done." Her perspective reminds us that reconciliation must be accompanied by a genuine commitment to justice and restitution, ensuring that those who have suffered are made whole.

Principles of Transformative Justice

Transformative justice extends beyond traditional legal frameworks, focusing on healing, empowerment, and systemic change. It involves several key principles:

1. **Restitution and Reparations**: Restitution involves addressing the tangible and intangible losses suffered by individuals and communities due to past injustices. This includes financial compensation, land restitution, and other forms of reparations. Voluntary restitution, where individuals or entities willingly contribute to reparative efforts, plays a crucial role in this process.

    Desmond Tutu, in his reflections on the TRC, acknowledges that "reconciliation without justice is a form of denial. We must be willing to confront the deep economic and social inequalities that apartheid left behind." Tutu's insight reinforces the need for justice to be more than a symbolic gesture; it must involve concrete actions that address the material conditions of those who have been wronged.

2. **Empowerment and Participation**: Transformative justice emphasizes the importance of empowering affected communities to participate actively in the justice process. This includes providing platforms for marginalized voices to be heard and ensuring that communities have a stake in shaping the solutions to their challenges.

    Prof. Barney Pityana argues that "justice must be participatory, allowing those who have been marginalized to take an active role in defining what justice looks like for them." Pityana's call for participation aligns with the chapter's emphasis on community-driven justice processes that empower rather than paternalize.

3. **Systemic Change**: Addressing the root causes of injustice requires systemic change. This involves reforming institutions, policies, and practices that perpetuate inequality and exclusion. It also means challenging and dismantling systems of privilege and oppression.

    Gareth Stead offers a Kingdom-minded perspective, stating that "systemic change requires a radical rethinking of how we structure our societies—aligning our governance and economic systems with Biblical principles of equity, stewardship, and justice." Stead's vision calls for a justice system that is not only restorative but also transformational, challenging the very foundations of systemic injustice.

4. **Healing and Restoration**: Healing is central to transformative justice, involving not just individual recovery but also communal restoration. This process includes psychological support, cultural revitalization, and the rebuilding of trust between communities and institutions.

    As **Robert Ntuli** highlights, "healing and restoration are not passive processes; they require active engagement with the wounds of the past and a commitment to rebuilding relationships based on trust, respect, and mutual understanding." Ntuli's perspective underscores the chapter's emphasis on reconciliation as a dynamic and ongoing process.

5. **Accountability and Transparency**: For justice to be transformative, there must be accountability for past wrongs and transparency in the processes that seek to address these wrongs. This includes holding

perpetrators accountable and ensuring that justice processes are open and accessible to all.

Michael Louis emphasizes that "accountability is the cornerstone of justice. Without it, trust in the system erodes, and the very fabric of society is weakened." Louis's focus on accountability aligns with the chapter's call for transparency and integrity in all justice processes.

Personal Reflections and Experiences

As someone deeply involved in social engagement and conflict resolution, I have witnessed firsthand the complexities and challenges of implementing transformative justice. My experiences as a mediator in conflicts, facilitator of community development, and advocate for social change have provided me with valuable insights into the practicalities of justice and reconciliation.

In my work with the KZN Transformers and Pioneers, I have seen the impact of addressing historical injustices through community-driven initiatives. The focus on holistic empowerment and systemic change has been instrumental in fostering resilience and transformation. This approach aligns with the principles of transformative justice, emphasizing the need for comprehensive solutions that address both immediate and long-term needs.

Reflecting on the South African transition, the negotiated settlement of our transition to democracy, while historic, left significant gaps in achieving full justice and restitution. The focus on political reconciliation, while essential, did not fully address the economic and social disparities that remain entrenched in our society. As **Prof. Pumla Gobodo-Madikizela** observes, "True reconciliation requires that we go beyond the narrative of 'forgive and forget' and engage deeply with the need for material and psychological restitution."

Empowering Change Through Restitution and Transformation

Transformative justice and reconciliation require a commitment to both restitution and empowerment. This means not only addressing the harms of the past but also actively working to build a more equitable and inclusive future. By integrating Biblical values, upholding constitutional principles, and embracing radical perspectives on justice, we can drive meaningful change and foster a society where every individual has the opportunity to thrive.

Conclusion

Navigating the path of transformative justice and reconciliation involves a deep commitment to addressing historical wrongs, empowering communities, and fostering systemic change. By drawing on Biblical principles, embracing the values of the South African Constitution, and integrating Kingdom-minded perspectives, we can work towards a future marked by justice, healing, and unity. As we continue this journey, let us remain steadfast in our pursuit of a more just and equitable society, guided by the principles of love, humility, and righteousness that underpin our shared vision for transformation.

Chapter 18: Revolutionizing South Africa Through Innovation and Creativity

In a nation scarred by historical injustices and plagued by enduring inequalities, the call to innovate is not just a whisper; it is a resounding demand for revolution. Innovation and creativity are no longer just desirable attributes—they are the lifeblood that must flow through the veins of a country on the brink of transformation or stagnation. This chapter doesn't just ask for change; it demands a radical reimagining of South Africa's future through the relentless pursuit of innovation and creativity. The stakes are too high for anything less.

The Imperative of Innovation and Creativity: A Matter of Survival

Economic Growth and Job Creation: Disrupt or Perish

In a world hurtling towards the future at breakneck speed, South Africa cannot afford to be left behind. The economic landscape demands disruption, not just adaptation. Innovation must become the engine of a new economy—one that does not merely create jobs but redefines the very concept of work. We need to disrupt industries, challenge monopolies, and empower the underdogs. The future belongs to those who dare to innovate, and South Africa must stake its claim.

Addressing Social Challenges: Innovation as a Weapon of Justice

Innovation must be wielded as a weapon against the systemic injustices that continue to oppress millions. It is time to use creativity to break the chains of poverty, inequality, and exclusion. We must design solutions that not only address but eradicate the root causes of social challenges. This is not just about incremental change; this is about flipping the script entirely, creating a new narrative where innovation is synonymous with justice.

Promoting Social Cohesion: Breaking Down Barriers

Social cohesion cannot be an afterthought; it must be at the forefront of our innovative efforts. The barriers that divide us—racial, economic, cultural—must be dismantled with the same precision and creativity that built the technological marvels of our age. Innovation must be the bridge that connects us, the common ground where all South Africans can come together to create a future that leaves no one behind.

Cultivating a Culture of Innovation and Creativity: A Revolution in Mindset

Education: The Battlefront of Innovation

Our education system must be revolutionized. We must wage war on the outdated, rigid structures that stifle creativity and critical thinking. Education must become a hotbed of innovation, where students are not just taught but are empowered to question, to disrupt, and to create. We must break free from the chains of traditional education models and embrace a future where learning is dynamic, interdisciplinary, and driven by the needs of the 21st century.

STEM Education as the Foundation: Science, technology, engineering, and mathematics (STEM) education must be prioritized, but not in isolation. These fields should be intertwined with the arts and humanities to foster a well-rounded, innovative mindset. Students should be taught to think critically and creatively, applying their knowledge to solve real-world problems.

Interdisciplinary Learning: We must encourage students to see the connections between different fields of study, to think outside the box, and to approach problems from multiple angles. Interdisciplinary learning should be at the heart of our educational system, preparing students to be innovators in whatever field they choose.

Entrepreneurial Education: Entrepreneurship should be a core part of the curriculum at all levels of education. Students should be taught not just to be workers but to be creators, innovators, and leaders. We must instill in them the mindset of seeing opportunities where others see obstacles and equip them with the skills to turn ideas into reality.

Supportive Environments for Innovation: Cultivating Radical Spaces

Innovation will not thrive in sterile, risk-averse environments. We must cultivate spaces where failure is not just tolerated but celebrated as a necessary step towards success. Innovation hubs must become the breeding grounds for the next wave of South African disruptors—places where the boldest ideas are nurtured, and the status quo is relentlessly challenged.

Innovation Hubs and Incubators: These should be established across the country, particularly in underserved areas, to democratize access to innovation. These hubs should provide not just resources but also mentorship, networking opportunities, and access to markets.

Public-Private Partnerships: Government, business, and academia must collaborate to create an ecosystem that supports innovation. This includes funding, policy support, and creating a regulatory environment that encourages risk-taking and experimentation.

A Culture of Lifelong Learning: Innovation requires continuous learning. We must promote a culture where individuals are encouraged to keep learning, adapting, and growing throughout their lives. This includes not just formal education but also professional development, online courses, and informal learning opportunities.

Leadership: The Vanguard of Innovation

Leaders must not just support innovation; they must lead it. The time for cautious, incremental change is over. Leaders at every level must become vanguards of innovation, driving their organizations and communities towards a future defined by bold, creative solutions. They must tear down the barriers that stifle innovation and create a culture where the best ideas can rise to the top, regardless of where they come from.

Leading by Example: Leaders must embody the spirit of innovation, demonstrating through their actions a commitment to creativity, risk-taking, and continuous improvement.

Empowering Teams: Innovation cannot be top-down; it must come from all levels of an organization. Leaders must create an environment where everyone feels empowered to contribute ideas, experiment, and take risks.

Recognizing and Rewarding Innovation: Organizations must celebrate and reward innovation, not just when it leads to success but also when it results in valuable lessons learned from failure. This creates a culture where innovation is encouraged and valued.

Leveraging Technology: A Radical Reimagining

Technology is not just a tool; it is the foundation upon which the future will be built. South Africa must invest in digital infrastructure, not as an afterthought, but as a critical priority. We must equip every citizen with the digital literacy needed to navigate and dominate in a digital world. Our tech startups must become the vanguards of global innovation, leading the charge in creating solutions that not only transform South Africa but set the standard worldwide.

Investing in Digital Infrastructure: Every South African must have access to reliable, high-speed internet and the digital tools needed to participate in the digital economy. This is not a luxury; it is a necessity for a thriving, modern economy.

Promoting Digital Literacy: Digital literacy programs should be widespread and accessible, ensuring that all citizens, regardless of their background, can take full advantage of digital opportunities.

Supporting Tech Startups: South Africa's tech startups have the potential to be world leaders in innovation. We must provide them with the resources, mentorship, and market access they need to succeed on a global stage.

Encouraging Grassroots Innovation: Power to the People

Innovation must be democratized. The most powerful ideas often come from the ground up, from the communities who live the challenges we seek to solve. We must empower grassroots innovators with the resources, platforms, and recognition they deserve. This is where the true revolution will take place—in the streets, in the townships, in the rural communities. It is here that the future of South Africa will be forged.

Supporting Community-Led Initiatives: Grassroots innovation must be supported, both financially and logistically. Local solutions to local problems can often be more effective than top-down approaches.

Inclusive Innovation: Innovation must benefit all segments of society. We must ensure that marginalized and underserved communities are not left behind but are active participants in the innovation process.

Fostering Collaboration: Communities must be encouraged to collaborate, share knowledge, and support each other in their innovative efforts. This collective approach can lead to more sustainable and impactful solutions.

Biblical Principles of Innovation and Creativity: A Divine Mandate

Innovation is not just a human endeavor; it is a divine mandate. The Bible teaches us the importance of stewardship, creativity, and the wise use of resources. These principles must guide our efforts as we seek to innovate in a way that honors our Creator and serves our fellow humans. Innovation is a sacred duty, a way to reflect the creativity of God in a broken world.

Solomon's Temple: The building of Solomon's Temple, as described in the Bible, is a powerful example of innovation, creativity, and collaboration. This grand project involved careful planning, the use of the finest materials, and the integration of diverse skills and talents. It serves as an inspiration for what can be achieved when innovation is guided by vision and purpose.

The Parable of the Talents: Jesus' Parable of the Talents is a call to use and multiply the gifts and resources we have been given. This is a clear directive to innovate, create, and not be content with the status quo.

Bezalel and Oholiab: The artisans Bezalel and Oholiab, filled with the Spirit of God, were tasked with creating the Tabernacle, a project that required the highest levels of creativity and craftsmanship. Their story highlights the divine inspiration that can guide human innovation.

The Way Forward: A Call to Arms

The time for complacency is over. We must embrace innovation and creativity as the driving forces of South Africa's future. This is not just about keeping up with the world; it is about leading it. We must become a nation of innovators, creators, and disruptors, committed to building a future that is as bold and dynamic as the people who call this land home.

Promoting Entrepreneurial Mindsets: We must instill an entrepreneurial mindset in all South Africans, encouraging them to see opportunities, take risks, and innovate. This requires education, support, and a culture that celebrates entrepreneurship.

Encouraging Cross-Sector Collaboration: Government, business, academia, and civil society must collaborate to create an ecosystem that supports innovation. This collaboration is essential for tackling the complex challenges we face as a nation.

Creating Inclusive Innovation Ecosystems: Innovation must be inclusive, benefiting all segments of society. We must address barriers to participation and ensure that all voices are heard and valued in the innovation process.

Building a Culture of Experimentation and Learning: We must create a culture where experimentation and learning are valued, where risks are taken, and where failure is seen as a stepping stone to success. Let us rise to the challenge. Let us embrace the radical, the revolutionary, and the disruptive. Let us build a future where innovation and creativity are the norm, not the exception. This is our moment—let us seize it with all the courage and conviction we can muster.

Chapter 19: Sustaining Community Engagement

Community engagement is the lifeblood of a thriving, democratic society. In South Africa, where historical injustices and socio-economic disparities have created deep-seated divisions, sustaining robust community engagement is crucial for fostering resilience and enacting transformative change. This chapter delves into the radical potential of community engagement, emphasizing principles of inclusivity, empowerment, and systemic change. By drawing from my experiences as a social engagement facilitator and leader, this chapter outlines transformative strategies for maximizing public participation, and underscores the critical role of a national dialogue in uniting all spheres of our nation.

Radical Principles of Effective Social Engagement

1. **Inclusivity and Radical Representation**: True community engagement demands radical inclusivity. This means not only engaging all segments of the community but prioritizing the voices of marginalized and underserved groups. Radical engagement ensures that these voices are not just heard but are central to the decision-making process. Every solution must reflect the diverse needs of the community, fostering a deep sense of belonging and shared ownership.
2. **Transparency and Accountability as Revolutionary Tools**: Transparent processes and accountability are not just administrative necessities—they are revolutionary tools for trust and empowerment. Openly sharing how community input shapes decisions transforms engagement from a superficial exercise into a powerful mechanism for real change. This radical transparency ensures that community members see the tangible impacts of their contributions, solidifying their commitment and participation.
3. **Empowerment for Systemic Change**: Empowerment goes beyond skill-building; it is about fundamentally shifting power dynamics. By equipping community members with the knowledge, resources, and confidence to challenge systemic issues, we transform them from passive recipients to active architects of change. This empowerment fosters a culture of self-reliance and systemic transformation, enabling communities to address their challenges autonomously.
4. **Collaboration and Partnerships for Collective Action**: Radical change requires deep collaboration across all sectors. This means forging strong alliances between government, civil society, and the private sector to pool resources and expertise. Such partnerships amplify efforts, drive

systemic solutions, and ensure that no community effort operates in isolation.
5. **Respect and Cultural Sensitivity as Foundations for Change**: Respecting and integrating the unique cultural contexts of communities is essential for effective engagement. Radical respect involves not only acknowledging but actively incorporating diverse traditions and values into engagement processes. This cultural sensitivity enhances the relevance and acceptance of interventions, making them more impactful and transformative.
6. **Flexibility and Adaptability in Dynamic Environments**: Communities and their challenges are ever-evolving. Radical engagement requires flexibility and adaptability to respond to these changes. Facilitators must continually adjust their strategies to meet emerging needs, ensuring that engagement remains relevant and effective in addressing the dynamic nature of community issues.

Radical Strategies for Maximizing Public Participation

1. **Revolutionary Needs Assessments**: Begin with a radical approach to understanding community needs. Engage with community members through diverse and innovative methods, such as immersive participatory research and real-time digital platforms. This thorough understanding lays the groundwork for targeted and impactful engagement efforts.
2. **Tailoring Engagement Methods to Diverse Communities**: Employ a range of engagement methods tailored to the unique characteristics of different communities. Utilize town hall meetings, digital forums, grassroots events, and unconventional methods to ensure broad and meaningful participation. This diversity in approaches ensures inclusivity and maximizes engagement across various demographics.
3. **Robust Feedback Mechanisms as Engines for Change**: Establish dynamic feedback mechanisms that allow continuous dialogue between community members and leaders. This includes regular feedback loops, public consultations, and real-time response systems. Actively addressing and incorporating feedback ensures ongoing engagement and responsiveness to community needs.
4. **Capacity-Building for Community Leadership**: Invest in comprehensive capacity-building initiatives that empower community leaders and members. Provide training in leadership, project management, and conflict resolution to enhance their ability to lead and engage effectively. This investment in human capital drives sustained and impactful community development.

5. **Sustainable and Impactful Initiatives**: Focus on initiatives that create lasting change. Implement projects that address immediate needs while also building systems and structures for long-term development. Sustainable initiatives foster resilience and ensure enduring positive impacts on the community.
6. **Ongoing Monitoring and Evaluation**: Implement a robust monitoring and evaluation framework to continuously assess the effectiveness of engagement strategies. Regularly review and adjust strategies based on outcomes to maintain relevance and impact. This iterative approach ensures that engagement efforts evolve in line with community needs and challenges.

The Revolutionary Role and Benefits of National Dialogue

1. **National Dialogue as a Unifying Force**: National dialogue serves as a revolutionary platform for aligning diverse voices and fostering a shared vision for the future. By creating spaces for inclusive discussions, we unite national priorities with community needs, driving cohesive and transformative change.
2. **Addressing Systemic Issues through National Perspective**: National dialogue provides a comprehensive view of systemic issues that local efforts might overlook. Addressing these issues from a national perspective ensures that solutions tackle root causes and drive widespread impact.
3. **Strengthening Democracy through Active Participation**: National dialogues reinforce democratic principles by encouraging active citizen participation and accountability. By involving all sectors in decision-making, we ensure that governance is truly responsive to the people.
4. **Promoting Social Cohesion through Understanding and Collaboration**: National dialogue fosters social cohesion by bridging divides and building solidarity. In a diverse nation like South Africa, dialogue helps overcome historical and social tensions, creating a more unified society.
5. **Driving Innovation and Collaboration**: National dialogues stimulate innovation by bringing together diverse stakeholders. This collaborative environment generates new ideas and strategies, leading to significant progress and positive change.
6. **Ensuring Accountability and Transparency**: National dialogues enhance accountability by providing a platform for public scrutiny. This transparency ensures that leaders and institutions are held accountable for their actions, reinforcing trust and confidence in governance.

Case Studies of Radical Community Engagement

Grassroots Movements as Catalysts for Change: The anti-apartheid movement exemplifies how sustained community engagement can dismantle systemic oppression. The movement's success underscores the power of collective action and radical inclusivity.

Community-Led Initiatives Driving Transformation: Initiatives such as the Abahlali baseMjondolo movement have successfully advocated for housing rights and dignity. These examples illustrate how community-driven projects can address specific needs and drive systemic change.

Actionable Steps for Individuals

1. **Becoming a Radical Community Leader**: Take on leadership roles by organizing community meetings, starting initiatives, or advocating for local issues. Become a connector who brings people together around transformative goals.
2. **Leveraging Technology for Engagement**: Utilize social media, online forums, and mobile apps to enhance community engagement. Technology can amplify participation, facilitate real-time feedback, and mobilize collective action.

The Role of Youth in Transformative Engagement

1. **Empowering Youth for Leadership**: Involve young people in community efforts by creating mentorship programs, youth councils, and platforms for their participation. Their fresh perspectives and energy are crucial for driving change.
2. **Educational Initiatives for Civic Responsibility**: Integrate civic education and community service projects into school curriculums to foster a sense of responsibility and engagement from an early age.

Intersection of Community Engagement and Environmental Justice

1. **Promoting Environmental Stewardship**: Engage communities in environmental justice initiatives to address issues such as pollution and conservation. Community-driven environmental projects can lead to long-term benefits and resilience.
2. **Supporting Sustainable Development**: Implement sustainable development projects that improve living conditions while protecting natural resources. Engaging communities in these efforts ensures lasting positive impacts.

Personal Reflections and Experience

My career as a social engagement facilitator has demonstrated the transformative power of community engagement. The challenges and successes I've experienced underscore the importance of radical commitment, flexibility, and collaboration. Witnessing communities take ownership of their development initiatives reaffirms the potential of participatory approaches.

Biblical and Ethical Foundations

1. **Ethical Leadership as a Revolutionary Principle**: Leaders must embody principles of integrity, justice, and service. Drawing from biblical teachings, ethical leadership involves shepherding communities towards the greater good and aligning actions with these values.
2. **Biblical Examples of Community Engagement**: Biblical stories such as the rebuilding of Jerusalem's walls under Nehemiah illustrate the power of collective action and radical community engagement in achieving transformative outcomes.

Future Vision for Community Engagement

1. **Reimagining Communities for Radical Change**: Challenge readers to envision communities transformed by full engagement and empowerment. Consider new forms of governance, innovative social enterprises, and inclusive public spaces.
2. **Building a Legacy of Engagement**: Emphasize the importance of creating a lasting legacy through community engagement efforts, ensuring that future generations continue and build upon the work done today.

Conclusion

Sustaining community engagement requires a radical and dynamic approach, characterized by dedication, inclusivity, and empowerment. By applying transformative principles, employing strategic methods, and recognizing the benefits of national dialogue, we can foster a participatory and cohesive society. Engaging communities in meaningful ways addresses immediate needs and lays the foundation for long-term development and unity. As we strive toward these goals, let us remain steadfast in our commitment to radical engagement, collaboration, and empowerment for the betterment of all. Through these efforts, we can build a South Africa that embodies the strength, resilience, and potential of its people.

UNMUTE COURAGEOUS CATALYSTS: *leading South Africa beyond historical trauma and fragmentation*

Lindokuhle T H Khoza

Chapter 20: A Call to Unmute Courageous Catalysts

As we reach the culmination of "Unmute Courageous Catalysts: Leading South Africa Beyond Historical Trauma and Fragmentation," we stand on the precipice of a monumental challenge. This book is not merely a compilation of strategies and insights; it is a resounding clarion call for radical and transformative action. It is a summons to rise as audacious leaders—courageous catalysts—who will confront the systemic injustices and historical traumas that have long plagued South Africa. Our mission is to blaze a trail toward a future of profound renewal and transformation.

The parable of the foolish and wise builders provides a potent analogy for our endeavor. The strength and impact of our efforts will be determined by the foundation upon which we build. Just as the wise builder anchors his house on unshakeable rock to weather the fiercest storms, so must we anchor our mission in immutable principles of justice, reconciliation, and empowerment. The path ahead will be laden with formidable obstacles and fierce resistance, but it is imperative that we remain steadfast. We must build on a foundation that will endure through every tempest and trial we face.

The Weight of Our Mission

Our undertaking extends far beyond addressing the challenges of today; it is about forging a legacy for generations to come. The youth and future generations are not merely observers; they are waiting for us to be the harbingers of change, the pioneers who will champion a radical shift towards a just, inclusive, and flourishing society. They look to us to dismantle the entrenched systems of inequality and oppression that have hindered progress for too long.

True courage means standing firm in the face of ridicule, opposition, and entrenched resistance. It means defying the status quo, challenging the powerful forces of inertia, and remaining resolutely focused on the broader vision of a transformed South Africa. Our nation carries the heavy burden of a legacy marked by division, injustice, and systemic dysfunction. Yet, it is precisely because of this weighty history that our mission is not just important—it is imperative.

The Vision of Transformation

Amidst the trials and harsh realities of our present, there is an exhilarating promise of transformation. As we embark on this bold mission, we will witness the metaphorical deluge of rain—a powerful symbol of sweeping change on the horizon. This rain signifies the outpouring of justice, reconciliation, and collective prosperity that will flood our nation, washing away the remnants of historical injustices and systemic barriers. It represents the surge of renewal and healing that will emerge as we boldly confront and dismantle the old paradigms.

Our task is monumental, but its rewards are profound. By unmuting courageous catalysts and grounding ourselves in a foundation of unyielding principles, we are laying the groundwork for a new era. This era will be defined by a resurgence of hope, a revitalization of community spirit, and the emergence of equitable prosperity. We must face the storms of resistance with unwavering resolve, ever focused on the transformative vision that lies ahead.

The Urgent Call to Action

As we close this chapter, the call to action is loud, urgent, and unambiguous. We are summoned to be the trailblazers who rise above adversity and remain resolutely dedicated to the grand vision of a reimagined South Africa. The transformation we seek will not be handed to us; it will be forged through relentless dedication, unflinching courage, and a commitment to foundational principles.

Embrace this mission with the awareness that the journey will be arduous and fraught with obstacles, yet rich with opportunities for profound and lasting change. Future generations are depending on us to lead with boldness, challenge the deep-seated systems of oppression, and usher in an era of justice, equality, and reconciliation. Our efforts will forge a new path for a society where the benefits of our labor will be manifested in the unity, prosperity, and dignity of our nation.

As we move forward, let us view the storms and challenges not as mere impediments but as opportunities for monumental growth and transformation. Let us rise with the conviction that the rain of transformation is not just a promise but an imminent reality, heralding a new dawn for South Africa. The call to unmute courageous catalysts has been issued—let us respond with unparalleled boldness, unwavering faith, and an unrelenting commitment to a brighter, more equitable future for all.

The time to build on rock is now. The time to lead with courage is now. The time to transform South Africa for the generations to come is now. The future demands our leadership, and it is our duty to rise to this challenge with unyielding resolve and boundless hope. Let us be the catalysts of change, and let the heavy rain of transformation pour forth and reshape our nation for the better.

www.ingramcontent.com/pod-product-compliance
Lightning Source LLC
Chambersburg PA
CBHW081617170426
43195CB00041B/2862